JOURNEY TOWARD ETERNAL LIFE—
ALASKA STYLE!

Among the Hair, Hide, Guts, and Feathers

ERWIN N. HERTZ SR.

InspiringVoices®
A Service of **Guideposts**

Inspiring Voices books may be ordered through booksellers or by contacting:

Inspiring Voices
1663 Liberty Drive
Bloomington, IN 47403
www.inspiringvoices.com
1-(866) 697-5313

ISBN: 978-1-4624-0371-4 (sc)
ISBN: 978-1-4624-0372-1 (e)

Library of Congress Control Number: 2012919112

Printed in the United States of America

Inspiring Voices rev. date: 11/01/2012

Thank you to those who helped me throughout the process of writing this book—which in itself is an answer to prayer.

Father Peter Gorges, a humble man of great faith, and an astute spiritual mentor who has been there for me throughout my adult life. There are others that have walked alongside on my spiritual journey. They may go unnamed, but not unappreciated. You know who you are.

Jeannine Erhart, a friend whose heartfelt commitment (for years) to transcribe my stories and God's stories, began it all.

Judy Dippel, writer and editor. She took on the job of revising and organizing my transcribed stories for this book, helping me to finish it. (http://www.jldwrites.com)

Beverly Jones, owner of Kings Store, Haines, Alaska—for her many months of efficient, enthusiastic help with emails, scanning and copying.

ENDORSEMENTS

"Erwin Hertz is a man of wondrous spiritual insight. Where others see coincidence or fate, Hertz sees the hand of a loving, caring, personal God."—Father Peter Gorges, Sitka, Alaska

"Hertz and I came to Alaska 50 years ago. In the town of Haines adventure is evident, and Hertz's life is a fantastic adventure story. We both have God to thank that either one of us survived."—Harold Hannon, friend, Haines, Alaska

"I have been friends with Hertz for 39 years, in the town of Haines, Alaska. Hertz is spiritual, kind, hardworking, funny—as hard as granite, though you usually don't see that side of him. Don't let his kind demeanor let you think Hertz is milk toast. He has had many jaw-dropping, rough-and-tumble experiences over his lifetime. Only through the grace of God could Hertz have made it this far. Take a walk with Hertz through the amazing stories of his life, and his spiritual growth. Buckle your seatbelt tight for this wild read!—Dick Flegel, retired banker, Haines, Alaska

"It is an honor to have known Erwin Hertz (since the sixties), and to know about his incredible journey with the Lord. After I returned from Viet Nam, I heard of all the miracles in his life. With God at the helm, he has been able to go through many of life's storms, from early childhood to present day happenings. This book will surely encourage you for more of what God has to offer should you be willing to take that step of faith while reading this book.

Be encouraged with this must read book. God helps Erwin; God can help you, too."—Gene Strong, a Promise Keeper brother in the Lord, Haines, Alaska

"I have worked with Hertz. He is the real deal, rough-and-tumble, but generous and kind. Read this book. You are sure to learn something."—David Swift, carpenter and fellow Alaskan

I dedicate this to the Lord Jesus Christ
This is his book, his miracles
Ask; he will answer

This verse changed my life forever
*Ask, and it will be given to you; seek, and you will
find; knock, and it will be opened to you.*
Matthew 7:7

The angel's quizzical expression on the cover of
my first prayer journal seems fitting . . .

The cover of this book serves as a reminder

But those who hope in the Lord will renew their strength.
They will soar on wings like eagles; they will run and
not grow weary, they will walk and not be faint.
—Isaiah 40:31 NIV

From inside the fish [whale] Jonah prayed
to the Lord his God.
—Jonah 2:1

CONTENTS

INTRODUCTION

There are two outstanding four-letter words that I keep in my heart and mind all of the time. One is **LIFE**, and remembering to be thankful for every single day that the sun comes up, and for every single day *I get up!*

And the second is **AMEN**—a beautiful four-letter word that I pray will surge from my soul and be spoken from my mouth frequently throughout each day of my life. Amen: so be it! Agreeing with God, and trusting what he says is true, is essential if I want to live a life of purpose!

I realized a long time ago, as I learned to appreciate the deep meaning of both LIFE and AMEN, that living each day with God, *and knowing I am loved by him*, makes forgiveness and good things possible. It's repeatedly clear I don't control a thing, except my choices in whatever life circumstance I find myself in. I've learned to see the world from God's point of view. He knows all. I sure don't.

In all honesty, this could be the beginning and end of my book. If you remember nothing else, I hope that you will open your mind and heart to the amazing grace of God and his unconditional love! He fills every believer, freely giving overflowing abundance in LIFE. Just ask; God will respond.

Jesus has brought me so far past what I am personally capable of ever being, thinking, or doing. He shocks me with his faithfulness, and I'm exceedingly grateful how I continue to grow. Every day I get to know him more. Writing a book is completely out of my element, nevertheless God has provided the way for me to put my life experiences, my faith, and personal adventures into words.

Through his unlimited love, power, provision, and authority my plea to accomplish this book has been heard, my prayers answered.

At 76, I've lived lots of life, maybe even more than my share! I could write three books of stories about all the people, experiences and events that lie within, and in-between, those two four-letter words. Each day I continue on with my life journey *toward eternal life*. I'm humbled by the good, undeserving blessings I've received which are more precious than Alaska gold. At the same time, I've also faced, endured, and overcome many circumstances in life that seemed impossible. With God, I've been able to carry on during the unexpected, unwanted, and undeniably hard and painful things that being a human being throws our way—the harsh realities of living life on this earth, for me *and* for you.

As an electrician, purpose and power are interesting and familiar words in my life, but they have increased in importance as God has allowed me to be a firsthand witness of *his* ongoing "purpose and power." His miracles and the answered prayers I've witnessed on this earth are beyond my ability to explain, yet I must openly share them.

I've owned an electrical company for over forty years in the small town of Haines, Alaska. I use my electrical contracting skills on the job, and when teaching others how to step into this profession. My days are spent with electricity, currents, conductive paths, circuits—all kinds of power and transformers, but nothing on earth compares to the transformation I've received through walking in the power of God, Jesus Christ, and the Holy Spirit. There's no going back, my life is changed forever.

I'm well aware that God often asks more of me than I feel able to do. I felt that way about writing a book. *Me? How, Lord?* But I know this is something God has asked of me. In his power, he has shown me so much of himself, so in obedience *to him,* here is my book—done!

As you read on, my prayer for you is that it will point the way to a closer connection to God, and stir up a craving for you to learn more about Jesus Christ's power and strength in your own life. He has healed, protected, and guided me in mine, and *I don't know why.* I believe it is because I ask, in faith, for what I need. I 'm just an ordinary guy, and a little rough around the edges, but the one thing I do know for sure is that he is the one and only son of God, and he loves *even me!* He sees that my prayer log is worn and falling apart. My Bible is disintegrating and God knows I'll buy a new one, and still treasure his words and my notes on the tattered pages of my old one.

The purpose of this book is clear to me. *I pray, dear God, my somewhat unique life experiences and relationship with you, will light the way for others to know you more. I know without a doubt, Jesus, that as people seek more of your divine presence, and ask what they need from you, your power and wisdom will guide them from here on out.*

This book shares my real life journey about love, self-acceptance, and includes my crazy adventures and humor—and most importantly celebrates God's miracles. All that is written within this book is to be used for his purposes. ". . . for thine is the kingdom and the power and the glory forever." Matthew 6:13

Amen!

Erwin N. Hertz, Sr.

PROLOGUE

HEALTH NUT AND HORSE PILLS

As the deer pants for the water brooks,
so pants my soul for you, O God.
My soul thirsts for God, for the living God.
—Psalm 42:1-2

May, 2004—Life events shake up the
ordinary days to help us see evidence of God
and his amazing acts of grace.
—Erwin Hertz

God saved *my hide* on an ordinary day.

"Hertz, do you want to go to Mother's Day dinner at the Halsingland Hotel after church?" David asked. David, his wife, Donna, and their daughter, Mattie, were currently living in the upstairs of my house, and going to dinner with them sounded good to me.

"Sure. I get out of church about a half hour before you, so just come by the house and pick me up."

I went to church, and when I got home I was feeling a little croupy and congested, so I took one of the big horse pills that Harriet Stall, who is a health nut like me, had given me. Those pills always give me a boost because they have a lot of Vitamin C and other good stuff in them. I knew they were gigantic, I'd taken them before. I didn't even think about breaking it up this time, since I'd never had a problem swallowing them.

Without a thought, I popped one in my mouth, took a drink of water, and it immediately got stuck in my throat. My throat was kind of sore already, and it firmly lodged in the area of my Adam's apple. I drank some more water and it wouldn't go down. It wouldn't budge. I could feel my throat swelling around it. I drank some flax seed oil that I had in the refrigerator, and it still wouldn't go down.

The predicament I was in, started to sink in after a couple of minutes. I thought, *maybe I should call the fire department.* I had retired as a volunteer fireman after twenty-seven years. I would have called, but I couldn't talk. (Not being up on technology, I didn't know they would see my phone number if I called.)

What can I do? I figured I had to do *something.* All kinds of things darted through my head. I felt like I should get out of the house. I thought that maybe I should go lay down in the road where somebody could see me—at least they would stop! That didn't seem too smart because I was definitely running out of time. Even though there were a few houses on my road, nobody was driving around at ten o'clock on this quiet Sunday morning. People on my street were still asleep. The clinic in Haines was closed on Sundays, and there wasn't enough time to drive there anyway. I already knew I couldn't talk, but suddenly I felt myself not being able to breathe! Logic told me I was out of breath, out of time, out of options!

Strangely calm, I decided to go out and lay down in the carport, where David and Donna could see me when they came back to the house. My carport was only twenty-five feet from the road, but with no one living straight across from my house, only a field of trees, no one else would see me.

I accepted what was happening—I was going to die. I could not breathe and knew I was close to being done! At least David and Donna would find me when they came home. Good for me, but I suppose not so good for them!

I walked out to lie down in the carport. It was May and about forty degrees. I'd said my prayers and written in my prayer book that morning. I remembered, very clearly, a verse in the book of

Psalms that I'm always encouraging other people with. It came to me. God said, "Call on me in your day of trouble; I shall deliver you." Psalm: 50:15.

And God's word tells us, people won't receive if they don't ask. (John: 14:13) I went to the carport to lie down. My life on earth would soon be over. As I went down on one knee, the ice cold of the cement penetrated. I was conscious of wanting to lie down, and of my prayers spoken to God earlier in the morning. I couldn't speak any words to God out loud, but they were in my heart.

From deep within me, my thoughts cried out, *Lord, Jesus please save me!* That's all. I was still down on one knee, and that big ol' horse pill was still firmly stuck in my swollen throat. It felt hard, and didn't move in the least. It was there to stay. Within seconds of my plea to God, I suddenly felt something in my mouth—it was the pill. I hadn't moved, or been jarred, or done anything, but there it was, in my mouth. Opening my mouth, it fell right out in my hand. It was still as big and solid as when I had first swallowed it—only four or five minutes ago.

I spit it out and threw it across the road. "Wow! . . . Wow!" I felt stunned, trying to comprehend what had happened. I'd spent those few minutes with that pill slowly draining the life from me. My throat was especially sore and raw where the pill had been stuck, but now it was out and I was alive! *Alive!*

I went back in the house in awe of the fact that scripture had come true that very moment in my life. It was a miracle, and I don't say that lightly—without question it happened to me.

I *had* asked. I *was* alive. This happened only because I had asked God, asked Jesus Christ, to save me! I was breathing normally again, and I was a happy, happy camper, who was on a complete spiritual high. I wanted to stay in the presence of the Lord and never leave it. Shortly after that, Dave and Donna drove in. I told them what had happened and they were in shock. I was too! (Chuckle of relief)

"I'm not going to go and eat with you. I feel so great that the pill is out of my throat and that I am alive." I encouraged them to go and enjoy themselves, and reassured them that I was fine. (Chuckle)

The peace I felt was amazing—I was *so grateful* to be alive! It was an absolutely fantastic feeling. To this day it is hard to describe. They went on and I stayed home, kind of floating through the whole day trying to comprehend God's act of grace upon me. I was so happy. I felt such joy—the presence of God, the Holy Spirit was with me in my house. There was a peace beyond my own understanding, and an incredibly personal time with God that I will never forget. Fantastic!

I didn't tell others what had happened; only Dave and Donna knew. I don't remember if I ate or drank anything before I went to bed that evening. I felt tired, and called it a night early, about 7 p.m., rather than my usual 10 or 11 p.m. While still awake in bed, the immense feeling of peace remained. I knew I was experiencing a spiritual reality—one of a living God, that is beautiful, secure, and often impossible to explain in words.

I conked out, and when I woke up, I looked at the digital clock on the dresser, and it read 2:30 a.m. Of all things, I looked directly up from my bed, and it appeared that there was no ceiling on the bedroom. Instead, it was as if I was outside, looking into God's creation and a clear midnight blue night sky filled with bright stars. It was gorgeous, clear and calm. I couldn't believe God allowed me to experience the wonder of his presence on that so-called ordinary day. It was anything but ordinary!

Abraham Lincoln once said, *"How can a man see the Heavens, and see the stars and creation, and not believe in God?"*

Man, I was so impressed about what God had done for me earlier in the day, and now to gaze into the heavens . . . I could not believe it. I relaxed, and then fell back to sleep in the joy and peace that surrounded me.

I woke up the next morning, still astounded. I headed off to work, but the reality of undeserved grace and the amazing power of God went with me.

The next Sunday when I went to church, I had to share what had happened. I told the congregation about the trauma, *and the miracle*, of the experience with the "horse pill" and the midnight blue sky, of incredible tranquility and beauty, that God had shown me in the middle of the night. Helen Strew, a good friend of mine, said, "Yeah Hertz. You take so much stuff that it would be just like you to die taking a vitamin pill!"

Like I said, LIFE is a four-letter word that is priceless.

PART ONE

MONTANA

"The Treasure State"

**Erwin Hertz lived in Montana from 1936-1956
Born in farm country near Charlo,
Montana—fifty miles west of Missoula**

We would cut holes in the ice so the cattle could get
to drinking water—One day, years ago, a $5,000 bull
fell through the ice and drowned—*not good!*
—Erwin Hertz

CHAPTER 1

ROOTS, BIRTH AND LIFE—THE ORDINARY AND EXTRAORDINARY

I planted the seed in your hearts, and Apollos watered
it, but it was God who made it grow. It's not important
who does the planting, or who does the watering.
What's important is that God makes the seed grow.
—1 Corinthians 3:6-7 (NLT)

God saved a wretch like me,
but I figured I had to start somewhere.
—Erwin Hertz

You, like me and everybody else, has (or had) a dad, a mom, and a place of birth. Like most of life's events and circumstances, we don't control whom we are born to or how or where we get to grow up. My family heritage and childhood were a mix of challenges to face and blessings to be grateful for. There comes a time in life for most of us when we realize that hard times and adversity builds character and makes us strong or discourages us and makes us weak. Throughout it all, I chose a lifelong journey of seeking God to help make me strong—physically, mentally, and spiritually. I've never been a perfect guy, but God is more than perfect, and, fortunately, early on in my life, his love for me was made crystal clear. You'll hear

3

about this and his amazing grace in nearly every part of my life story. It's not much of a story without God—he makes it extraordinary!

I was raised in a Catholic church, and, from an early age, I wanted to learn to say a "perfect prayer." That desire was the beginning of a continuous process of learning about who God is, what he could do, and how he kept getting my attention to help me get to know Jesus Christ and the Holy Spirit up close and personal. God's hand and his forgiveness has been with me all of my life, as long as I sought after his will and asked for his forgiveness. However, I'm getting ahead of myself. For now, come with me back to my growing up years.

Even as a young kid, life was never dull. I was always busy with lots of responsibilities and work on the family farm along with opportunities for plenty of mischievous play. My growing up days were ordinary (for all I knew), with the extraordinary slipped in, and the harsh and ugly rising up here and there.

From day one, and still today, I've lived in states that are bigger than life—breathtaking, rural and rugged landscapes like farm and small town life in Montana and Alaska, isolated from the hustle and bustle. Western Montana's glacier country was where I was born (with the help of a local midwife) to August and Albertina Hertz on August 3, 1936 on a share-cropping farm in Cross Place, near Charlo, Montana, not far from Missoula. At the time of my birth, my father was a sharecropper. We had an outhouse and no running water; he wired simple electricity, first at the barn, then at the house. That came before other modern conveniences.

The Charlo area is still a small community of hardworking farmers and cattle ranchers. It is definitely "big sky" country where sunshine sparkles off fish-filled rivers and lakes in the summertime, and herds of deer and elk thrive, even though harsh winds, rain, and snow (about fifty inches a year) influence life on every level in the wintertime. The area is bordered by several protected areas, including the Herak Waterfowl Production and Ninepipes Reservoir. Even today Charlo has only around 500 people, and the 4th of July parade and cookout are the biggest events in town. After leaving there, I've lived in Haines, Alaska since 1961, so I've never been a city boy, except during stints offshore when I was in the Navy.

Overall, I grew up with good parents. My mom was a loving, responsible, nurturing, and protective woman, big and strong like a mother-bear. She liked to laugh, and she prayed for us and was the "heart" of the family. My dad was a forceful, hardworking, physically powerful, disciplined, and emotionally undemonstrative German. I felt my dad was a cut above the rest. I never had to ask, "Who is in charge?"

Soon, the sharecropping farm became our family farm, and it eventually grew into several farms and a working ranch in Montana. From the time I was born, hair, hide, guts, and feathers were part of my life, and, after moving to Alaska, that heritage and style of life continued. I don't live on a farm today, but hunting, fishing, sports, and the wild outdoors fill my days.

> Animals with hide, tame and wild, have always been a big part of my life. In fact, I'm surprised I haven't grown hide myself.

Oddly, I didn't walk until I was two. When I was older, my mother told me she was upset about it, because carrying me all the time was a chore. It was not easy with all the work she had to do. I had two older brothers, so, somehow, I must have known that with the first solid steps would come work on the farm. One of my first jobs, at about four years old, was to keep the wood box full; it was a tough job in the cold Montana winters.

Early on, I needed to get strong and thick-skinned. (Seriously, a natural grown hide would have helped.) The wood shed was by the barn, about forty yards from the house, and the wood box was on the porch of the house. It had to be full year-round because wood heated the house in wintertime, and all of the cooking was done on the wood stove, all of the time.

One January day, when I was older, about five or six, I had been goofing around and didn't get the wood box filled. My dad got me up at midnight. He demanded, "Get up and fill the wood box."—dressed in my boxer shorts only. He wouldn't let me put on other clothes, not even shoes. My feet had chronic frostbite while growing up because none of us had the right shoes for the 40-below, snowy, icy weather of Montana anyway. It only took me one time to learn, *happiness is a full wood box.*

At five, when I wasn't much bigger than a five-gallon bucket myself, my other job was to keep an eye on the milk buckets in the barn. I was supposed to tell my older brothers when they needed to be changed out so they wouldn't run over onto the floor. It was a full-size job because we had thirty-five Holsteins, and they had to be milked twice a day. I rarely got help from my brothers because they were never close by. They were busy milking cows and changing the milking machines from one cow to the other. So, to me, it made sense to lug out the full five-gallon milk buckets by myself. On a strict German farm, I tell you, you *did not* spill the milk! It was a bad thing to spill the milk, so I got strong and determined at a young age. The old saying, "There's no use crying over spilled milk," was true most of my childhood. If I didn't do things just right, I took whatever consequences my dad dished out. He could be a pretty hard-nosed task master. However, I attribute much of my success in how I cope with and overcome many of life's challenges to him—that's not a bad legacy to leave a child.

After my dad's first two wives, came his marriage to my mother

My dad, August "Gus" Hertz, and his first wife had two boys, my half brothers—Richard, in 1930, and Eugene, in 1931. They were married for a short two years, and she died when the boys were only one and two years old. Dad really struggled to make a living working on a farm with his two little boys to care for too. He had a second marriage that I just recently found out about. He married his first wife's sister after his first wife's death. They were only married for five months, and she also died. I can't imagine how tough that was on my dad. In fact, some people suspected foul play and thought he may have killed the sisters. Of course, that wasn't true, and some years later they found out something in the two sister's family medical history had caused their deaths.

In 1934, Dad married his third wife, my mother, Albertina Doll, who was born in Glenullian, North Dakota. My mother's parents were Clemms Doll and Rosa Keller-Doll, both born in Katherinenstad, Russia.

My parents on their wedding day

My mother, Albertina, took care of Richard and Eugene even before she married my dad. My parents spoke German most of the time in the early years to each other, but eventually had to speak more English to us at home so we could learn it for school. I have an older sister, Loretta, who was born in 1935, one year before me. I was born in 1936, my brother Duane was born in 1942, Clem in 1947, my sister Linda in 1951, and Douglas in 1956. I was in the middle of the family, *no man's land!*

My dad's roots and farm blew away in the "Dust Bowl"

The farm that Dad worked when he married all three times was in North Dakota. He lived and farmed there in what some people called the "Dirty '30s." This horrible period of severe dust storms is something most of us know about but didn't experience. Hundreds of thousands of people were forced to leave, the soil blowing away beneath their feet. Dad was one of them, and 1934 was one of the worst. Severe drought, along with decades of extensive farming, caused the soil to dry out and turn to parched dust.

The soil on Dad's farm literally blew away in large dark clouds. The Dakotas were nothing more than a useless dust bowl. My dad went broke and lost everything, just like a whole bunch of other people did in those years. He had to get out of there, so he borrowed a little money and headed out with his two work horses, Lady and Dick. He loved those horses, probably because they were so valuable to his farming. With them, and little else, he boarded a freight train for Montana.

One event on the train stands out. He told me, "One night on the train these two rough guys threatened me, tried to rob me and throw me off the train—I found a two by four." That was all he ever said. All I know is that he was on the train alone after that—he made it to Montana, they didn't! I didn't want to ask what happened to the two men that had tried to rob him, and he never mentioned it again. One thing I do know for sure, my dad was never scared of anybody in his whole life—not that I could see.

It was 1934 when he returned to desolate North Dakota, married my mother, and brought her and his boys out to Montana. Dad went from place to place trying to find land to scratch out a living. He had no money, but he had German-American pride and persistence. I watched those characteristics take him a long way in his lifetime.

> God gives every bird his worm, but he does not throw it into the nest. —Swedish Proverb

Finally, just after I was born in 1936, he came across a farm in Montana owned by a man named

Hutspet. He was older, and also a carpenter. He couldn't keep up with the dawn to dusk work on a farm. Dad struck an agreement to cultivate and run the farm and sharecrop with him. The place belonged to Hutspet, but the word was that the land had never produced so well, or been so well taken care of as when my dad worked the farm. Probably because he had gone hungry a few times in his life, Dad was more than eager to work hard to make this farm succeed and thrive for both of them. It was a hard going, because the place was very primitive. There were a couple buildings, a house and a barn, but no electricity or running water. Eventually it became our family farm, and the land we all grew up on near Charlo.

We planted deep Montana roots, and dad created new opportunities that increased his success throughout his lifetime. He founded the cattlemen's association, transporting the community cattle on railroad directly to Omaha buyers—more lucrative than going through a middle man that would come up to Montana to buy cattle.

This annual event was followed with a big party celebration in the fall. Even in his senior years, Dad loved to Polka. After my mother died, all the gals would dance with him at the community gatherings—*he would always have a heart attack the next week!* This went on for many years, and at eighty-three he did pass away from a heart attack. He was a pragmatic man, and had chosen to go off his heart medications. He felt better, so it made sense to him to accept how this would all play out for his long-term health!

On his way to the doctor one day, Dad had gotten a haircut and laid out his suit—I guess he knew it was his time, and it turned out that it was! I couldn't talk to him about God, he would just walk away. But in his later years I sent him the book, *Beyond Death's Door.* After he died, in the back of the book, he had written down what he had to do, personally, to have eternal life. Though we hadn't talked about it face-to-face, this gives me peace knowing he accepted what God offered, and is resting in peace with Jesus.

I knew more about my mother's faith in God. When she died at 73, many years after a stroke, I never questioned that she rested with him. I loved both my parents, and did see my dad's love in action when he cared for my mother at home (with the help and support of other family members) the last years of her life.

Outward shows of affection, by word or deed, was not part of my dad's personality, but he was a good man

Survival set the priority for everything that my dad did in my growing up years. Energy was not put into a life of comfort and convenience like we know today. Dad wired the barn first, even before the house, because lights and milking machines for the cows were more of a necessity.

For some time, the cows were milked by hand, by the light of lanterns. After milking, the milk was strained and poured in the cream separator. I remember my mother cranking that separator by hand; the cream was dumped from the top. It worked pretty slick—one side the cream flowed out and the other side skimmed milk poured out. Cream was a great way to make money. Dad didn't sell the milk, but one of my brothers did have a dairy farm later on. I was sort of surprised he ever wanted to see another cow! It was a tough go, with lots of hard work for all of us kids in those growing up years.

I didn't know my dad. All I knew is that he worked a lot—farming, fixing, building—he was a handyman extraordinaire. I guess at the very least you would call him an industrious, inventive German craftsman. I admired him, and so did others. (He made a machine that was like a hay bailer before the hay bailer was invented. Too bad he didn't patent it, but all he thought about was what was needed to make the farm work easier, more efficiently and faster. That was his passion, his every day priority.)

But I could never talk to my dad. He never had time. He did talk to my oldest brother, Richard, because he was like Dad's foreman for the farm. With work always the priority, Dad told Richard what fields to work, what tractor or piece of machinery was needed behind the tractor. I wasn't in that category. I felt like I was one of the invisible, voiceless ones that just did what he was told. I was sort of jealous of Richard—I felt like he was Dad's favorite, but now I see it was because he could do the work. I never did want to do all that he had to do—it was hard, and it had to be done exactly as Dad told him. He had to be fast, and his work was expected to always be done right.

Richard had lots of adult-sized work pressures, causing him to have ulcers by the time he was in high school. Eugene, my second oldest brother and I would get in trouble, and Richard would have to kick us back into shape to make sure things got done according to Dad's instruction. Even though I always felt being a middle child was "no man's land," I'm glad I wasn't the oldest or the youngest in the family. My youngest brother, who was the last one to leave home, ended up stepping in where Richard left off, and there was nothing easy about it.

My Dad, nicknamed "Gus," was one of the first farmers around to buy a tractor, which helped the farm to produce even more. He knew how to plant, when to plant and irrigate, where to put ditches in the field, and precisely when to harvest. Dad rented some Indian land to raise more grain, so the work only increased. He irrigated it and that was one more responsibility.

One time when I was about seven years old, I went with him to turn on the water to fill the ditches for irrigation. He showed me how to open the water gate that let water flow into a culvert. Dad went down to change the dam where the water came from; it was way across from the field. He warned me, "Do not walk across that other field over there because it is not ours!" We didn't know the other farmer that owned it. "You have to walk around it on the road."

I hiked myself up to where I could pull the rope to open the water gate. Pretty easy task! After I finished opening it, I didn't see anyone in the other man's field, so I decided to take a short cut across it, probably two-hundred to three-hundred yards.

I was about half way through the field when I saw the farmer that owned it. The man had his dog with him, and he sent it after me—*and it was big!* I tried to out run it, but couldn't. It kept barking after me, biting my legs, nearly knocking me down. About then, the man called his dog back. I finally got across the field with torn up pants and chewed up legs, and lots of crying and tears.

I told my Dad what happened, and all he said was, "I told you not to go across that field!" He was right. Even so, that is one time I remember wishing my dad could have talked to me with a little bit of empathy. I guess his ability to show emotion towards me (and the other kids) didn't work quite right, and maybe needed some fixing!

My dad—I admired how he could fix things and make them work on our land and in the house

Dad was a good, hardworking man—otherwise I didn't know him.

He did a lot of electrical work around our place, but he wasn't a trained electrician. He was self-taught. When I went into the Navy and became an electrician and got back home, I realized how bad Dad's wiring was. *Wow!* Not sure how he got everything to work, but he did. He even began to wire electricity for other people, since everyone around there lived like we did. Apparently what you don't know won't hurt you!

We had a cement cistern. Water was hand pumped from it to fill buckets and take to the house and for the water we hauled over to the barn to water the pigs or cattle, or whatever other livestock we had. Like so much of my dad's resourcefulness and inventions, I was always in awe and amazement. Dad just could do it—he was a force that always did whatever "it" was.

Since we had lights and a hot water heater in the barn before we had hot water or lights in the house, every Saturday night we pumped and hauled water for my mom to heat on the stove. We all took take a bath in the washtub in the middle of the kitchen. The rest of the week we just had to wash our feet before we went to bed and call it good!

I always wanted to be the first one in the bath, because the water was nice and hot, but everybody else wanted the same. When it got down to the last person to bathe, the water was lukewarm and icky grey looking, but it was normal for us and it didn't seem weird.

Though it might have been tough at times, I wouldn't trade my childhood for anything! I attribute our first-rate farm (and the later success of several farms and a ranch) to my dad's ingenuity. The co-op, grange, and a cattleman's association were all created due to his resourcefulness.

In 1942, at six years-old and living way out in the country, I still remember when the Japanese bombed Pearl Harbor. The news spread like wildfire. My mother would sing, "We didn't invite you over, but we are going to repay the call!" Another verse that she sang I can still hear in my head, "There's no place like home, the fire is out and it's 42 below, there's no place like home!"

North Dakota's winters were similar to Montana's, and because she had come from a family of twelve girls and two boys, survival was dependent on the girls working the fields. She was lucky to be big and strong at five foot ten, because she had to work like a man for her family. My mother was a big, tall, and beautiful gal, even when she worked in the fields with overalls on. Women only wore dresses back in those days. I guess German women are strong-willed, practical and independent; at least my mom was—because she had pants on and thought nothing of it! Those old farmers were sure impressed with my mom. There just wasn't enough hired help available outside of the farm to run it, without some of the girls taking on a load of the farm work. That's just the way it was.

> I learned this truth at an early age: God does not give you a life that makes him unnecessary.

When all eight kids were old enough to go to school, we had to walk about a half mile to catch a bus to ride the other six miles to school. *No, I didn't have to walk the six miles through snow, sleet and hail*—but when we did get home from school we did have feeding and chores to do for the beef cows, milk cows, pigs, brood sows, feeder pigs, and chickens.

For fun, we went hunting from a very young age. In time, we had five farms. Geese and pheasants flew through them on their way to Canada in the spring, and back through again as they flew further south in the winter. Today, the sound of geese honking, and to see them wing their way through the sky, take me back in time. We lived in bird hunter's paradise—fun adventures and great eating.

In the years growing up we spent all the time we could hunting, fishing and riding horses. It doesn't get much better than that for a guy like me. After all, hair, hide, guts and feathers are made by God to provide for specific needs in life, and we had more than our share—plenty!

What a man, my dad! All my life I admired him, but I didn't think he loved me—the bottom line, I didn't love myself

I finally told my dad I loved him after I had two children of my own. Even then, he couldn't say the words, "I love you!" It just wasn't in him to be able to do it, but when I told him it softened our relationship, made it better. After that, we enjoyed many good years. I felt much more connected as father and son, and I think he did, too. I'm very grateful for those last years.

With God's help, I learned how to love myself, along with more eye-opening experiences than I can begin to put on paper. I think you will be amazed by some of the stories of God's intervention in my life as you read on. *Thank you, Jesus!*

I want you to get to know my dad, and how he spent his days improving the farm. It's foreign to many. I've always said he excelled because he was a steadfast, unwavering German man. Can you imagine digging a well in clay soil with hand tools? That's what he tried to do, out by the barn. What a job. He hired another guy to help with the digging, since he was spending much of his time making money selling cream.

They started by digging out a cavity, five foot in diameter, in the clay soil. It gave them both room enough to stand and dig. They dug down quite a ways, something like seventy to eighty feet, digging only by hand and shovel. It was a terrible job and proved to be impossible. I can still see the huge pile of brown clay that they hauled over by the barn!

What eventually happened was that the well began to cave in after they got down that far; Dad realized it had gotten too dangerous to continue the day he almost got trapped in one of the cave-ins. He didn't want to pay the money to have a well-digger come in, but he had no choice.

It took days of work, even with the well-driller. Even he had to keep pounding and pulling, pouring water down to soften the base, then keep pounding and pulling continuously with the drilling devise. Finally they hit water and was that ever a happy day for all of us on the farm! I will never forget the look on my dad's face and how ecstatic he and the driller were, because as it turned out it was a couple hundred feet down before the hit water. No easy task, but oh, happy day!

And were we kids ever glad, too, since we pumped and hauled water all the time to keep the farm and animals with water—it was one more piece accomplished to help efficiency so that the farm could prosper. Since the well couldn't be pumped by hand any longer, they had to put some kind of electric pump in the well. *Hey, good deal*—there were no complaints from us kids.

Dad got quite a reputation for having ingenuity and skills that could help other farmers out, not only with wiring their barns, but with plumbing, too. He was in big demand—he never seemed to slow down, just kept going, always working hard. Life on the farm just got better and better. Hutspet loved the increasing crops and livestock, and Dad began to lease more land to farm.

My Dad's family—for the record

Growing up, you might have already guessed, we never talked about my dad's family. In a German family, anyway this one, you didn't ask a lot of questions—no point, because they would not get answered. My dad, August (born in Glenullian, North Dakota) had two younger brothers, Frank and Joe, and two older brothers, Phil and Pete. Phil was his oldest brother and he owned a bar in Mandan, North Dakota. Pete was a cross country truck driver; I think he lived in Oregon. Joe was in the army in Dutch Harbor, Alaska. Dad had three sisters; Eva, Katherine and the other's name I can't remember, since very little was ever said.

My father's father died when Dad was in the third grade—my grandfather, Achanasius Hertz (born in Leonopol, Russia) was a veterinarian and only forty years old when he died.

I always had a feeling in my heart that Dad had gone hungry growing up, and with no one to help them out, it was something he never forgot. I believe that made him unbreakable, and drove his intense desire to work endless hours to keep food on the table. He was a survivor! Church was the one thing that could stop his continual working. Every Sunday of his life, he would dress up in a suit and a tie, all of us boys would too, and we would go to church as a family. He didn't talk about that at home either!

Grandma Rose

My dad's mother's name was Rosa Mosbriscker (born in Felsenburg, Russia). She was a power-house in the family. When I was growing up, she would come by train from North Dakota to Montana to visit us in the summer. To me it seemed that she was four feet tall and four feet in diameter. She was a force through-and-through! When she visited, she would kiss us and pinch our cheeks between her thumb and forefinger! It hurt, so we soon learned to hide on the barn roof when she arrived so she couldn't kiss us and grab our cheeks. (Chuckle.)

She would ask my parents in German, "What are those kids always doing on the barn roof?" In between her English sentences, we kids thought she was cussing in German. But we could make her laugh, and we got a kick out of her—that made us feel good because she was a very stern, hardworking woman. She read her Bible, cooked, cleaned, canned, and ran a farm back in North Dakota. Unfortunately, when she visited she never read the Bible to us and she never prayed with us. I wish she would have.

Grandma Rose had a hardwood cane, and she had a fast, strong grip with it that grabbed at us to hook us in. With each other, we kids called her "the hooker." In a flash, she would whip out her cane, flip it up, grab the end of it and hook it around our neck and jerk us right in. Then she would take the cane off our neck, and *whap-whap-whap* us with it on the head, hollering, "Go fill the wood box!" "Why are your clothes dirty?" "What are you doing?"

But we loved her because it wasn't boring when Grandma Rose came to visit. Sometimes I wondered if she had *whapped* all my dad's emotion out of him with that cane over the years (chuckle). Or maybe it was because my dad's *own dad* died when he was so young, that losing him like that caused him to rein in his own emotions his whole life. Who can know—my father was just the way he was . . .

By now, you can probably guess that Grandma Rose and my mother were not good at being in the same kitchen. My mom mumbled to herself, upset with her much of the time. It was Mom's kitchen, but Grandma Rose wanted to run it . . . "yes ma'am" . . . and she *always* made soup. Still, I can see in my minds-eye—two strong-willed German women, apron to apron.

Most of the time Grandma's soups smelled good and tasted pretty good, too. We didn't always know the ingredients—they often remained a mystery. Her soups simmered with whatever happened to be in the garden; strange herbs, and with other unidentified weeds that grew around the place. Grandma knew what we didn't—I guess she would be an esteemed Master Gardener today, since I'm still alive to talk about it!

My brother, Eugene, would come in the house and say, "Oh no Grandma, soup again?" She would say, "*Ya,* soup again!" But she would say it in German. It was so funny—I can still hear her clear as a bell! Then she would add, "Soup makes you live ten years longer!" Right then in my life, I wasn't worried about living ten years longer. Even though it was good, we wanted something else, *anything else,* besides Grandma Rose's soup.

As the story goes, "back in the day" her famous sauerkraut soup saved many lives during an epidemic in North Dakota. Even so, I admit, I could not swallow down some of her German concoctions—so I did kind of a quick sneak in, taste and run—had that maneuver down pretty good, at least before she could get me with her cane!

Now these next details aren't for those with weak stomachs. She made use of skunks, too. She skinned the hides to sell, so a crock of skunk fat always showed up with Grandma. "What?" you're saying. Yes, it's true.

And when we got sick she rubbed the skunk fat all over us—a common remedy used by Native Americans, *and our German Grandma Rose!* Believe me I never wanted to tell her I was sick again. I got well fast. I'm not sure if it was the skunk's fat that cured me or my will!

And for our continual frostbite, she would put our feet in the hottest water we could stand, mixed with horse manure. No need for incense, when we had sauerkraut, skunk oil and horse manure—those did the trick! Again, I apologize if this is offensive to your senses; for Grandma Rose her remedies made good sense. That's my family for you!

PRAYER and FAMILY

"You are the children of those prophets, and you are included in the covenant God promised to your ancestors. For God said to Abraham, 'Through your descendants all the families on earth will be blessed.'" Acts 3:25 (NLT)

Me, my family and yours, need the hand of the Lord on us every day and every night.

Have mercy on us, Lord, and give us your protection, forgiveness and grace. I plead this in the in the blood of Jesus—let it be over us, every day. Thank you for restoring your blessing and redeeming each of us who ask. We hold you up on the cross—fill us with your Holy Spirit. I ask this in your holy name.

Thank you, Jesus. Amen.

CHAPTER 2

THE LOVE OF GOD: PERFECT PRAYER—IMPERFECT LIFE

> And now abide faith, hope, love, these
> three; but the greatest of these is love.
> —1 Corinthians 13:13

> What does love have to do with
> faith and prayer? As a child, I didn't know.
> I had never been told I was loved, and I didn't
> necessarily feel loved. Anyway, no one ever said
> "I love you" to me, until . . .
> —Erwin Hertz

Love is such an important word, but not one I heard spoken about as a child. The Catholic nuns in church may have talked about God's love in their teachings, but all I remember from early on, in catechism, was their instruction on how to pray. (By the way, they didn't live an easy life, and they weren't pushovers; they were tough and fun—I liked them; they even played baseball and other sports with us farm boys; quite a sight!)

Seriously, they were powerful in prayer. I respected the nuns, and all I knew was what they taught, because back then, we didn't individually read the Bible at church or home, and a mix of English and Latin was spoken in the Catholic Church when I was a child.

My mom made sure we went to confession once a month. Early on I didn't really even know what to confess. But before junior high, I realized what I needed to confess—I had plenty. (I didn't crack open a Bible and read it myself until I was in the Navy. A stint in the service is enough to make anyone's innocence go out the window—I knew I needed God's word to help me big-time by then!)

As a family, we all went to church on Sunday. It was just a little one-room church out in the middle of a field. There was no excuse; we had to be really sick to miss church. My mom liked us to "fast" before we went to church, and she also was the one who made sure we were clean from our Saturday night bath. Dad, my brothers and I dressed in suits and ties, with shoes always shined. Mom and the girls wore their best dresses—we all looked pretty fancy, but in those days, a person didn't go to church without wearing their Sunday best.

But you guessed it—we didn't talk about church when we got home. Other than my mother telling us that she was praying to God for all of us kids to grow up and be priests and nuns, I didn't know much else about any of it—I went through the motions, doing what was expected, and of course thought I should want to be a priest.

> In first grade, I told my brother, "I bet you $100 I will be a priest!"

From my early training at church, and my mother's dedication to rosary and prayers (maybe from my own feelings of being unworthy within the family), I somehow got it in my head that it was very important for me to say a perfect prayer, and my "Our Father's" and "Hail Mary's." All this was pretty hard to do since I wouldn't have recognized a perfect prayer if I'd said it—at five I didn't know what it really was—probably because there isn't such a thing as a perfect prayer from imperfect human beings. I didn't know then that God didn't demand perfection, but simply wanted my sincere heart. Sorry to say, I didn't learn that in life as soon as I would have liked.

The nuns told us that we should always pray before going to bed at night. For a tired farm boy, I can tell you that isn't the best time! But at five years old, I tried very hard to do what the nuns taught.

My two brothers slept in a double bed on the back porch and I slept in a single bed. They would be sound asleep and I'd lay in the dark, night after night trying to say a perfect prayer. "Dear God . . . Our Father . . . ," and time and time again, I would wake up the next morning, disappointed, because I had fallen asleep and hadn't said a perfect prayer—much less even finished a prayer.

I frustrated and let myself down over and over again trying to say a perfect prayer. This went on for several months. Another morning, another sunrise, another disappointment in myself that I didn't stay awake; I didn't feel I could say a perfect prayer. I tried again the next night, and the next, but my perceived failure in praying just right hammered home to me that I couldn't do it, and that I was imperfect. My strict German upbringing and normal insecurities continued to make me feel less than my brothers. At least I should be able to pray the perfect prayer, but I couldn't!

So much for achieving the perfect prayer, but years later, at 10 years old, I learned about God's everlasting love, and came to understand and firmly believe deep in my heart that I was loved by him and that "If God is for us, who can be against us?" (Romans 8:30-32)

I had no clue that a big God event was about to happen on an ordinary day—and what better place for God to make his loving presence known in my life than when I was going fishing? On this eventful day when I was 10 years old, I hopped on my bike and met my three best buddies (all brothers). We rode down the road meeting up with two other of our buddies. Then we headed a few miles further out on our bikes to get to this great little creek to fish for trout.

It was really hot, so we stopped at this itty-bitty country store that was along the road. We turned in all the pop and beer bottles we found along the way, and got enough money to buy a few cold pops to drink. I was the last one to go into the store. All my buddies were sitting beside the store. I went in, bought a pop and came out, the screen door closing with a clap behind me.

Walking out, I looked over toward the hay field by the store. It was mowed, and a big wide open space. I saw a guy standing all by himself in the field. He seemed to be looking intently right at me, so I climbed through the fence and went over to talk to him, curious about what he was doing there. I don't know why I did what I did, but God did. He had a purpose.

I was dressed in my usual farm kid clothes, but this man's clothes looked kind of odd for our area. He was dressed in casual clothes, but not dressed at all like a farmer. Little did I know that God was about to not only let me see this man, an angel-person, but also allow him to tell me something very important. Only I could see him—my friends couldn't figure out what I was doing in this low grass and field. They hollered and asked, "What are you doing?" Nothing in the field interested them, because they couldn't see what I could see.

I kept walking over to this guy, and the first thing I noticed in his face was that he had absolutely the clearest, most distinct blue eyes; they were just beautiful—I felt he was looking right into my soul. It was startling! Then, and all these years later, I know he was no ordinary person. He began to talk directly to me about the love Jesus Christ had for me. That truth amazed me. Nobody had ever told me that Jesus Christ loved me! In fact, nobody had ever told me *they* loved me. I was sort of confused, and at the same time so relieved and glad to be told I was loved by Jesus. My life started to change right then. God had a purpose for me and my life that I wish I'd picked up on sooner.

I looked over to where my buddies were by the store; they still had no clue why I was out there. They began to hop on their bicycles to head down the road to catch some fish. I told the guy that I had to leave because my buddies were leaving and I wanted to go with them. I don't exactly know how I knew at the time, but it was clear to me that I had seen an angel of God, and been told something valuable I would never forget—that *Jesus loved me!* I had been given a gift—an angel of God spoke to me, orchestrated by the pure and loving grace of God. He got my attention, (even though during a difficult season at fourteen, I unconsciously would not accept his unconditional love for me.)

I have wondered about that event many times over the years, and always wished I would have picked up and acted on the love of Jesus Christ then, and grown much stronger in my faith at a much younger age than I eventually did. I guess I'm like most people, relationship with God matures in stages; it is a growing process throughout all our years on earth. Even so I am thankful, *very thankful* that God gave me tangible awareness of his love so many years ago. I never will forget it, even though it was many years later before I would fully accept it. I had been given a great gift through that brief moment with an angel in a field—the knowledge that he loves me, that I could hold on to during the ups and downs of my growing up years—and firmly instilled in me for the rest of my days.

Oh yeah, by the way, there are perfect prayers, but only those that Jesus prayed. One example is found in Matthew 6: 9-13. "Our Father who art in heaven, hallowed be thy name . . ." I know, without a doubt, that all of my life, God has honored my intense need to try and say a perfect prayer when I was a young child. It took me awhile to understand that God didn't want my focus to be on creating a perfect prayer—he wanted my focus to be on getting to know him, to love and worship him!

After coming to realize that I didn't have to say a perfect prayer, the next step in my journey was to build a relationship with God, and to know I was loved unconditionally by him. I didn't have to try to work harder to earn more of his love. Why? He loved me already, no matter what, just the way I was—"by grace you have been saved through faith, and that not of yourselves; it is the gift of God." Ephesians 2:8

Being told by an angel of God that Jesus loved me was my first vivid knowledge of God's living presence and grace in my life. Yes, imperfect me! Boy, he got my attention in a way I never could have imagined in my wildest dreams!

JESUS PRAYED THE PERFECT PRAYER
—Matthew 6:9-13

I learned to never take this verse for granted. God's power is with us all the time—we must use it, not abuse it.

Pray, then in this way: "Our Father who art in heaven, hallowed be thy name. Thy kingdom come, Thy will be done, on earth as it is in heaven. Give us this day our daily bread. Forgive us our debts, as we also have forgiven our debtors, and do not lead us into temptation, but deliver us from evil. For Thine is the kingdom and the power and the glory forever. Amen."

CHAPTER 3

HOPE FOR HOPELESSNESS

For you are my hope, O Lord God; You
are my trust from my youth.
—Psalm 71:5

I know that God has a purpose for all of us, but as a kid
that didn't always register. I didn't feel I had any value
within my family. I didn't feel loved.
—Erwin Hertz

This is a painful subject, but I need to talk about it because God provided what I needed. He knows my life story, he knows yours. The remedy for despair is available to all of us—it is found in God, and in acknowledging his unconditional love for us—a love that can miraculously replace the heavy, bleak, darkness within our soul with hope and light.

I pray by sharing this that it helps other people—just by knowing that at fourteen years old, I had such a sense of hopelessness that I held a pistol to my head. I am thankful that over the years I have been able to help other people because I experienced that lonely, desperate feeling—I almost committed suicide.

When I was in this dark depression, I had a feeling of complete hopelessness in life and in my circumstances. I didn't know my awful feelings would pass, that feelings and circumstances change, and rarely stay the same. I didn't grow up in a family that was "hopeless."

I didn't understand that concept; it was totally foreign and not even acceptable in my family's vocabulary.

Yet, unfortunately, I believed the lies of hopelessness that Satan fed me, rather than remembering the unconditional love God had for me. He had let me know I was loved by him (spoken to me through the man-angel in the field) when I was ten years old, but for a short time as a teenager I didn't remember it.

It was kind of odd, because when this incident happened I was only in the eighth grade. I had a lot of friends, people liked me and I was popular in school. I don't know how this feeling of hopelessness and dark depression came over me, but I feel it stemmed from feeling unloved within my family.

I always had felt my dad didn't even like me; for sure I didn't think he loved me. I knew that my mother loved me, but still, I felt worthless because it was so important that my dad give me some signal that he loved and valued me. He never did, so as a kid I felt lost within my family, just one more kid wandering around; the fourth from the oldest of eight kids in my rigid German family.

As I said earlier, I liked the farm we lived on, greatly admired my dad who worked hard all his life to go on to purchase four farms and a ranch. My only explanation for getting into such a dreadful state of heart and mind was that I was wrapped up in myself (who isn't at fourteen?). Seriously, my self-centered thoughts were probably my biggest sin at the time. What I didn't know then, is that only thinking about myself was not getting me anywhere, but only making me feel worse and more isolated.

Within me, the thought process that I seemed to have went something like this: I wanted to do something to make my dad feel bad, because I felt really bad that I wasn't loved by him. Somewhere inside me I thought that my suicide would get his attention, and at the same time, take away my feelings of uselessness, worthlessness and hopelessness.

My folks never said that they loved any of us. Now I know that is true in other families too; I just didn't know that then. First and most important was work—Dad worked whenever he wasn't sleeping; first one farm, and then on to more farms. Hopelessness wasn't an emotion to ever allow or openly admit, and for my German father or mother to say "I love you," no never! Love wasn't expressed in word or action by my dad (my mother loved me, I know). I forgive them. It wasn't their fault, because I don't think their folks said "I love you," to them either. Thankfully, I survived that desperate, emotionally isolated time in my life. Anyone can survive it; you can, it's just a matter of choosing to look up and trust God. He meets us right where we are.

I've experienced so much good in life, and learned so much about God's grace along the journey of life, I wouldn't trade it for anything. Even though I suffered through the horrendous thoughts of suicide and almost acted on them, God didn't allow it to happen.

For me, that eventful day happened near our home farm. We had a field on one side that bordered the railroad tracks. On the other side of the tracks was a region of the country called the "Badlands"—familiar to me, but a devastated area of land.

It got that way long ago, when the railroad was cut through the hills, leaving piles of dirt and rock. It's a land of hills, not green and lush, but sparse, covered in piles of dirt, rock and sagebrush. The Badlands couldn't be farmed. It wasn't a good place to raise anything, except the beautiful wild horses that were plentiful. It was out there in that desolate land where we often hunted, that I held a .22 pistol to my head. It seemed to me like the right time and the right place.

I'm reminded as I write this today that suicide is nothing but an extremely poor and totally wrong, misguided choice, even though it sometimes feels to anyone in that state of mind that it's "easy to die, but hard to live." By looking to God, (not the world), and the authority of Jesus Christ and the wisdom and guidance in God's word (what he says), we are saved in this world and for eternity. Looking to him, takes away the confusion and brings truth to our suffering, and love and healing to our innermost self.

How did I have access to guns when I was so young? I began shooting when I was about eight years old; grew up with .22 rifles and pistols for hunting pheasants, ducks, geese and deer. Our whole existence, as kids, was to go hunting and fishing whenever we had time to set out and find pheasants, ducks, geese or deer. We hunted other birds that ate with our chickens. We hunted ducks that landed in our grain fields as they migrated south from Canada in the winter. They really ate up the grain fields—the wheat, barley, and oat fields mostly, and whatever grain was left from harvest.

This story about hunting is a bit of a rabbit trail, but earlier in the season they would land when grain was still on the stalk; they could flatten and destroy a grain field in a hurry if we let them, so we would shoot them and eat them. Mallard green headed ducks, man, they were beautiful ducks . . . and they were really good eating. I remember how we would sometimes go out in the dark to sneak up on ducks. You could hear them; they sounded like a feathered army, quacking and talking to one another.

One night, we crawled in to get up near the ducks. It was getting dark and they couldn't see us, and we couldn't see them. We climbed under the fence, and suddenly we jumped up, and in seconds, all the ducks took off. The sound of loud ducks in flight is loud; a bird-like jet plane taking off, with noisy ducks and wings everywhere! I guess you could say they were in quite a flap! I have lots of great memories of ducks, and duck hunting, on the Montana farm.

As kids we had guns available to us because we had a lot of problems with gophers and badgers digging holes in our fields, too. When we were irrigating the fields, the water would run down into their holes and cause sink holes. We boys trapped or shot the gophers, and got five cents for every gopher tail. We saved that money up and we were happy as clams being able to make some money. It was normal farm life—it may sound harsh to those who never lived that life or hunted, but it's the way it was.

> If you begin to live life for God who is all around you, every moment becomes a prayer.—Frank Bianco.

At fourteen years old, as I began to enter high school, my thoughts of suicide remained even though the sun came up every morning and life went on. I do not know what I was thinking, except everything felt completely hopeless. I didn't want to go to school.

I wasn't too bad a student in grade school, once I got the swing of it, but high school as a freshman frightened me.

The class voted me in as class president. I was scared! I didn't want to be president of the class. What does the president of the class do, anyway? I had no clue! So why on earth did they vote me in as president? They must have liked me, but I quit school for a short time because of them voting me in as class president.

When I went back to school, I got into trouble and got kicked out. Finally, I came home and told my dad that I had quit school. (Read more about this in the chapter: "A Dozen Things I Learned on the Farm," #5)

To sum it up, my dad never said one word to me about quitting school, but starting the next morning he told me to begin work in our rocky field, picking up and stacking rocks all day, every day. I did do this for a couple of weeks. One day, I told Dad, "I think I will go back to school." My news probably came as no surprise to him!

I am so thankful that I went back to school, but I still didn't know what my problem was—I couldn't shake my depression—didn't have a name for it, didn't know that's even what it was, but I was as dull as ditchwater; sick at heart. So one gloomy day in the fall I walked down there, beyond the end of our farm, past the lake, across the railroad tracks, into the Badlands, way out where no one would see me, and maybe never even find me, and held that .22 pistol to my head. I was very upset, disillusioned, and even more depressed and disgusted with myself now that I was sitting out there with thoughts of killing myself. I didn't know what to do; I was desperate, felt I had no other choice, and literally had no one to talk to about how I felt.

But I thank God every day that I loved my mother, and that he brought her to my mind at that very moment on that hopeless, bleak day so long ago. She was the key to my hope and survival and God knew it. For years, she was the only reason that I stayed at home. Suddenly, I knew that it would absolutely break her heart if I killed myself, and even then, I knew I couldn't stand for her to have to feel that way—I couldn't do that to her. She was a good, kind person, even though she would thump us on the head once in a while when we were growing up. But I did know she loved me, even though she didn't say it. It's not surprising that it was only my dad who gave us spankings with the strap if we didn't get home in time to do our chores, or if we did something wrong on the farm, or broke something. I remember it well.

> **Yet the righteous will hold to his way,**
> **and he who has clean hands will be**
> **stronger and stronger.**
> —Job 17:9

One thing God helped Job see, and helped me clearly see, is that it is totally selfish to commit suicide. I was only thinking about myself, no one else, especially not my family, and I had to stop it. Being depressed makes any of us vulnerable to the lies of the enemy. Please pray these following verses, and talk to someone you can trust if you are struggling with depression or thoughts of suicide. Talk to someone now.

> **Attend to my cry, for I am brought very low;**
> **Deliver me from my persecutors,**
> **for they are stronger than I.**
> —Psalm 142:6

Destroying our life, the one that God gave us, is more than a lie of the enemy, it is sin, and we do have a choice. Hopelessness is temporary—I pray right now that you never believe you are helpless or hopeless—*never ever!* I learned that powerful truth. I know that spiritual warfare exists; we can only fight it effectively by calling on God, and by standing firm on the word of God. Also, it is important to recognize that often we can face spiritual warfare when we begin to seek and draw closer to God, and when we begin to do good works for God.

Satan wants nothing more than to wreak havoc on believers and come between a strengthening, growing, building relationship with

God. Praise God, because he's given us power over all that confusion and destruction! He saved me from myself when I was fourteen. Jesus died to give us power over lies that destroy us. God knows. God hears. God cares. God preserves life—yours and mine.

> **Because the foolishness of God is wiser than men, and the weakness of God is stronger than men.**
> —1 Corinthians 1:25

Now I know without a doubt that God loves me, but I didn't know it back then. I am thankful, today, that God let me go through that time of depression in my life. Since then, people have crossed my path that felt they wanted to commit suicide, and through God's grace, I have been able to help them. Some were back in my younger years in Montana, and others after I got out of the service and moved to Alaska. I have been fortunate to befriend people who felt isolated in Alaska. It can be hard up here, when away from family and support. I thank God that he is able to use me when someone feels they are in a desperate situation—to offer a glimmer of hope. God is faithful and amazing to show up and help people move forward from there!

One man's success story

I was riding my bicycle in Haines, and I met a young man on the road. He had a look of sadness and hopelessness on his face. I said, "Are you okay, or do you need help with something?" He looked like he was going to cry. He was out of money and out of hope. I suggested, "Why don't you just stay here and I will come back and get you."

I took my bicycle home and got the car and went back down and picked him up. I got him a room at the motel and paid the nights rent. I went back and talked to him. He was feeling totally defeated!

He did not think that anyone cared about him. I told him that I would help him get in touch with his family and get back to them.

I talked to him about God and prayer (and I was not a prayer warrior at that time), yet during the couple of hours I spent with him, his hopelessness was replaced by God's inner hope and peace. Prior to meeting and talking to him, he was completely defeated and had lost all hope in life and his circumstances—he was right where I had once been as a teenager.

I'm still so thankful I was able to help this stranger make some phone calls and get in touch with his family. They loved him, and they were in shock about how he was feeling, where he was and what he was doing. He left town and reconnected with his them. He came back a few years later. We developed a relationship, and I could talk to him and pray with him. All I can say is that I'm so thankful for each person I've been able to help, and grateful that with God I was able to help myself all those years ago.

Lastly, I have to tell you, I felt kind of shook up about whether I should put a chapter about suicide in this book—tell the world about me sitting out in the Badlands, where no one would have found me, with a pistol to my head. I have to say it again: I was consumed in only me, and in selfishness. I want to impress that upon you, too. I don't say this to be critical of you or anyone, but to share a truth from the core of my being. Suicide is selfish! The only one that gains from suicide is Satan who is alive and well! Just look around our world! We have another option as we seek help from God and the people we can trust around us.

> ## GOD IS LIVING HOPE
>
> "Blessed be the God and Father of our Lord Jesus Christ, who according to his abundant mercy has begotten us again to a living hope through the resurrection of Jesus Christ."—1 Peter 1:3
>
> Later in my adulthood, God impressed on me to organize a prayer chain, which has allowed me to see what happens, again and again, when people ask God to come into their lives; to seek help, and discover his peace and love. He offers all of these to you, and so much more!
>
> *Lord, help us confess our sins; help us talk to you, listen to you, and believe in your love for us. Take care of us when we cannot seem to do it. Give us your peace (love and joy), which surpasses all understanding. Guard our hearts and minds through Christ Jesus.* (See: Philippians 4:6-7)
>
> *In Jesus name, I pray. Amen . . . hallelujah!*

This quote from, *Life after Life,* by Dr. Raymond A. Moody and Elisabeth Kubler-Ross is one to remember. It says, "as soon as we examine suicide from the standpoint of religion, we immediately see it in a true light. We have been placed in this world under certain conditions for the specific purposes, but a suicide opposes the purpose of his creator . . . God is our owner. We are his property. His providence works in our good."

Beyond Death's Door, by Maurice Rawlings, M.D., is a book that I've shared with many people since the early 1970's. It is good. God is good.

Chapter 4

A Dozen Life Lessons I Learned on the Farm

Blessed is everyone who fears the Lord, who walks
in his ways. When you eat the labor of your hands,
you shall be happy, and it shall be well with you.
—Psalm 128:1-2

Don't do what I did, do what I learned!
—Erwin Hertz

It's the little things in life that teach us. I learned dirt not only had to be washed off, but on a farm it was a priceless commodity. I learned some bugs were a nuisance, some harmful, others helpful—and *some even tasty*. And I definitely learned to appreciate that I was not the only son born to my father. I cannot imagine how hard that would have been!

Lesson One: My parents needed to speak less German and more English.

Early on in my life, my parents often spoke German to each other, but spoke English to us. The German language was the norm in their former North Dakota community, but proved to be a problem when my two older brothers went to school in Montana, where speaking German didn't work so well.

> **I learned** to, *"always remember that problems have improvement potential."*—Norman Vincent Peale

I started grade school in 1941-42. Even though it felt Dad cared more about the farm, he did want his kids to go to school. It wasn't talked about, but we all knew that he quit school in the third grade and started farming because his dad died at forty years old. I can't even imagine that, but I suppose since he made it pretty well in life without much school, he probably thought all of us kids could too, anyway if we had to.

My two older brothers, who were born in North Dakota in a more prevalent German community, were in the first grade for *only* three years when the teacher finally told my folks they needed to speak more English at home so they could get the boys moved out of the first grade and onto second!

When relatives visited, they would all speak German. We could understand most of what they said, but we didn't speak it. The two languages were really confusing for me, and obviously for my two older brothers, but at last my folks began to speak more English at home. It was important to speak the language of the country we lived in, even though later when I went into the military, after World War II, I wished that I could speak fluent German.

Lesson Two: The farm work came before education for all of us kids

> **I learned** to, *"knock the t off can't."*—George Reeves

My dad was share cropping his first farm, and then he started working another farm from land he rented on the Indian reservation. It goes without saying that we always had plenty of work to do after school. And depending on the season, sometimes we didn't even go to school for weeks at a time because we had to get the crops in or finish extra chores around the farms. The farm couldn't fail!

I was always so proud of both my dad and mom. They overcame everything and could do anything! And since school was not that important on the farm, I didn't really care about it either; I struggled with it. Fortunately, the Irish neighbors with the farm next to us believed formal education was important, even though most of the families from Ireland that lived in our area of Montana worked in the Butte Mines, often till they died. Their wives and the kids, for the most part, would run the farms, but they still knew education was important for their kids. That rubbed off on me some.

I always liked to go over to our neighbors, the Driscoll's, even before I started school. Lawrence Driscoll, their oldest child, who was now a big huge, young Irish man, was a great guy. I can still see him in his suspenders, milking cows in the barn. He would pick me up and throw me way up the air, and sometimes hoist me up on a nail, with my suspenders, on a post in the barn so I wouldn't get in the way of the cows. I was not much more than a toddler and I thought that was pretty fun. The Driscoll's were really great neighbors. God placed good people in my life that left a lasting impression.

My first grade teacher, Ann, was new to the area when I started school, and Lawrence Driscoll married her. That made her special in my book. She helped me in first grade, and believe me I really needed a lot of help. Even with help, I still flunked. We were supposed to be able to count to one hundred before we started school, and I don't think I could even do that, much less write the numbers—not a good start! (In her eighties, Ann Driscoll came up to visit Alaska on a tour boat. When it ported in Haines; we got together, reminisced and laughed all day.)

I never did like school, went most of the time, but I liked it better when we got to stay at home and work on the farm. I waded through school, probably like many farm boys who couldn't get their mind on it, or understand the purpose for it. Mom made me go but couldn't help me since she was so busy with her chores on the farm. My older sister, Loretta, was a good student and did help me, but I still got a "hit and miss" education as I halfheartedly plodded on. It reflected on everything I did later in life. When I had my own kids I knew that school had to be a high priority, along with athletics and friends—and living a life filled with God's best for them.

Lesson Three: *Geronimo!* I loved horses, and learned they were not only valuable on the farm, but great friends and lots of fun

I learned, *"enthusiasm finds the opportunities and energy makes the most of them."*—Henry Hoskins

My older brother, Eugene, was an expert rider. Like him, I was a horsemen; we had inborn enthusiasm and ability for horseback riding. My older sister, Loretta, was the girl in the family who liked to ride. At eleven years old, she had quite a scare riding a mare when a stallion showed up one day—there's more to the story, but I'll leave it at that.

We had saddle horses and work horses. The work horses were for pulling wagons, hay rakes, hay boats and buggies. The saddle horses were herding horses. Since we grew up with horses and guns, we didn't think much about accidents that could happen with either. (Later, I dated girls on horseback; also got into rodeo competitions. Horses were a big part of nearly everything I did.)

My horse, Geronimo, was a colt born on the farm—we grew up together. I'd ride bareback most of the time. I'd just grab his mane, jump on and we were gone! He was a red sorrel with a flaxen mane and tail—and he just kept growing and growing and growing. *He got huge!* I rode him all the time when he was little so he would be familiar with me when it came time to break him—*lucky for me!*

I fell in love with that horse. He got his name because when I rode him I had to cry out "Geronimo!" He was strong, fast and powerful . . . he could jump anything, herd everything—which he did, whether it had *hide* or *feathers*. He had "horse sense" about many things. Also, he was an animal that did mischievous stuff to keep from being bored!

Geronimo and I got into "horse wrecks" more than I can begin to tell you about. I'm glad I survived all his escapades with me on his back. Some of the mischief I got into was because of him. He was my best friend who led me astray. (Chuckle)

He followed me around like a big dog. He would nip me when I wasn't paying attention to him. Once he picked me up with his teeth, by chomping on to the muscle in my back, then he slammed me into the ground. He took off running down the field. For sure, he was a real joker, but he was always a best friend and an even better horse.

As I got older, we were allowed to go to a movie now and then—a huge treat! We went into town about fifteen miles from the farm. It cost us whoppin' twelve cents to get into the movie. John Wayne movies were big then, along with Roy Rogers and Gene Autrey.

We played good guys and sheriffs, bandits and robbers on horses. We would hide out on our horses in the trees at the river bottom, chase after each other, shooting our BB guns at each other. They sometimes went through our skin, but we could dig them out. Once I was shot right under the eye. Ended up with just a black eye, but these were not smart antics!

We tried all the cowboy tricks we saw in the western movies. We would jump off the barn and land on the horse and go galloping off. We learned it was best to do our jumping onto the horses without a saddle—the saddle horn really hurt when we landed on that! We never lacked for fun and adventure. And on our spirited horses we knew better than to shoot a rifle or shotgun off of them; only BB guns. I loved the adventures, and learned something new every day. It warms my heart when I think of those times now. Young boys, horses, the outdoors and vivid imaginations—nothing compares with what I learned from my boyhood experiences, horses and all.

Lesson Four: A strong work ethic—whether I wanted it or not, was engrained from birth

I learned to, *"hitch my wagon to a star."*
—Ralph Waldo Emerson

When I was about five years old, Dad was taking a fence down on the Hutspet's sharecropping property. The two work horses, Dick and Lady, were hitched onto what we called a "hay boat." It was built low to the ground so that we could toss on hay bales. It was about eighteen feet long and eight feet wide. It had runner planks underneath like a sled, but with two cast iron wheels on the back, each one three feet in diameter. In the hay field, it slid along easily; it was nothing for those two big horses to pull. Worked great!

On this day, my dad told me, "Hold the reins." He was taking fence posts out and throwing them on the hay boat to haul off. All I had to do was stand there and hold the horses reins so they wouldn't drag as the horses slowly pulled along. Dad "clucked" to the horses and they moved forward. They were in sync.

> My dad pulled the reins, said, "Whoa!" and they stopped! But those horses didn't do that for me!

I was so young, I couldn't drive them or stop them with the reins. Dad was walking right beside me and the hay boat. But a problem came . . . there was barbed wire laying on the ground from the fence he was taking down, and of all things to happen, the hay boat ran over this wire where the fence posts used to be. The wire began to shake the grass way out in front and back of us. The horses spooked. Dad saw it, but he couldn't jump on fast enough. In a flash Lady and Dick took off on a dead run with the hay boat and me attached—they ran a couple hundred yards with me flailing along behind. I couldn't hold them with the reins! I was bouncing around on that thing trying to stay on and hold onto the reins, but I couldn't. They were running *fast*; the hay boat bounced along and ran over this big ditch, flipping me off into the ditch, right in front of a cast iron wheel. It ran over both of my legs. *Ouch!*

My dad had to catch the horses. Once he got them stopped, he came back and got me out of the ditch. He knew my leg was broken, but what else was hurt he wasn't sure. He couldn't leave me in the ditch while he went to go get help, so he took me out, and as he did, the bone in my leg awkwardly and painfully rubbed together where it was broken. We were way off on one end of our farm, so he had to leave me while he ran over to a neighboring farmhouse that was closer than ours. Dad and the neighbor came back in a car. They tried the best they could to hold my leg as they put me into the back seat; they wanted to keep the bone from tearing through the muscle. It hurt every time my leg got jarred or moved, especially when they drove the car right across the bumpy plowed field to take me home. It was the best they could do, but a painful injury for a young kid.

The closest hospital of any size was in Missoula, fifty miles one way. That was a long drive in those days, so they packed my leg with pillows and took me to the hospital there. A doctor set my leg and put a cast on it. I had to stay in the hospital for a week because they wanted to watch for any other damage that might have happened when the big wheel rolled over me. The neighbor and my dad had to get home to the cows and chores. I was scared to death in the hospital by myself, and had a painful broken leg to boot. I cried a little bit; I guess it was called for—but there was good news soon. I was okay otherwise, no other injuries.

It got better for me when the word got out. After I got home, neighbors began to stop in and bring me toys and candy. Those visits and gifts brightened me right up and made me feel lots better! My cast went clear up to my thighs to stabilize the bone. I'm not sure how long I had it on, but it seemed like a long time to a little kid like me. I didn't go back to the hospital to have it taken off. My dad must have talked to the doctor on the telephone because finally he began to cut off about six inches of my cast every few days with a saw. (At least I hope he talked to the doctor.) At last it was completely off, and I was one happy camper! I learned on the farm that accidents happened, but work went on!

Lesson Five: Athleticism was a plus in school—agility, running, competiveness, and aggression

I learned, *"Before you can win, you have to believe you are worthy."*—Mike Ditka

My first year in high school, I was not a good student—not too surprising. I didn't want to go to school, but my mother made me. I had already flunked the first grade and the fourth grade—it didn't seem I was cut out for it! My record of scholastic achievement was definitely lacking!

But I could run—I set a record in the four-forty that stood for years—like all things, some years later, it was broken. My short-lived "claim to fame" served its purpose for me in high school. You might say, being an athletic farm boy "saved my bacon," and kept me in school. I did finally graduate. In our little town, the whole high school was only about seventy kids. It was a class "C" school in sports.

I felt sorry for the kids that grew up in neighborhoods in town, because to me, they didn't have anything to do, and weren't as fast and strong in sports—whereas on the farm we worked hard, had horses to ride, hunting and fishing to look forward to. We thought we had it made, shooting, riding, and racing tractors, along with anything else we could come up with—we weren't lacking in our desire to find wild and crazy stuff to do.

As I told you earlier, freshman year, they voted me in as class president. I did not understand what that meant or what I would have to do—I didn't want it. The idea of it scared me so much that I quit school. It intimidated me. I didn't feel worthy to be a leader or head of the class.

> I never felt I was the
> pick of the litter!

I didn't really know what was wrong with me, or why I felt that way. I couldn't talk to anyone about it, so I went home and told my dad I had quit school. He didn't say one word. The next morning he sent me out to one of the farms that had good soil, but had tons of rocks. (The state would haul off our stockpile of rocks to use for building banks.) Every day, after milkin' I picked up rocks, from early in the morning to late at night, and then milked the cows when I got home.

After a few weeks, I said to my dad, "I think I'll go back to school." Again, he never said a word—he knew what he was doing, but I didn't have a clue. At least when I went back I wasn't president! By my sophomore year, I found a passion for football, and I took all of my strength, aggression and frustration out on the football field—oh, my gosh, I loved football—*thank goodness!*

My whole existence and excitement about going to school centered around being able to play football. Even though I was a fast runner, I still sat on the bench when I played as a sophomore. Me and my friend, Rich, were chomping at the bit to play. One game we were getting beat badly, I guess the coach figured he had nothing to lose by putting us in. We stopped the other team; no more points got on the scoreboard after we went in. At the line of scrimmage we blocked or tackled everybody that came at us, and the crowd just went wild! I'll never forget it—we felt like sudden heroes, even though it was too late to turn the game around. The next game, we both were on "A Team." We played pretty well and started winning more games.

Football lit me up—I loved it! It kept me motivated to stay in high school. There's lots more learned from being a player on a sports team than some people realize. It served a positive life purpose for me. I'm so glad! Being competitive in sports was a way for me to learn how to move forward *and* survive life at the time. The sport and being part of the team gave me much more confidence. I was already into dating girls by my sophomore year, and being on the football team was a great way to be noticed and meet more girls. A real big plus as I began dating more seriously!

I played basketball in high school too, but I learned that it wasn't a good fit for my personality—I took it on like football, so I stayed on the "B" team . . . I always fouled out. I never quite got the hang of what the coach tried to teach me, *"Steal the ball. Don't jump on him!"*

Lesson Six: Creative Entertainment—kid fun could lead to danger and accidents . . . and trouble

> **I learned,** *"you have to do your own growing no matter how tall your [father] grandfather was. "*—Abraham Lincoln

Brothers, and my good childhood friends, Billy, Rich and Archie would come over, all three of them on one horse from their neighboring farm a couple miles away. Billy was always *driving.* Thinking back on it, I'm not sure how we survived our antics and mischief growing up. Maybe it was because our other good friend, Clarence, was more mature. His dad had been killed from an accident while working on the Grand Coulee Dam—Clarence had to grow up faster than the rest of us, and take on more responsibilities that weren't easy for a kid.

Or maybe it was the fear of my dad that kept us "in check." My friends and I all endured spankings from my dad's strap that hung on the back of the door; I knew that was part of the deal, and just the way it was. My friends did too. After I grew up and visited back at home, I'd hear stories from all kinds of people about the crazy things we'd done as kids—some true, some a bit false or exaggerated.

We were just farm kids who were into doing all kinds of adventurous stuff, but thankfully we grew up all in one peace, *kind of!* We jumped off barns onto the horses backs, leaped off cliffs into the river, just ourselves or sometimes on horseback. We had lots of freedom with guns and shot lots of birds and game, fortunately not each other. We raced horses, cars and motorcycles. You name it and I probably have a story to tell you. We would put on cowboy chaps and played in donkey basketball games. Boy, those donkeys could bite, kick and buck. We had the hoof and teeth marks to prove it!

But as teens, my buddies and I did land in a jail of sorts from a day of illegal pheasant hunting. After all, the pheasants ate with the chickens, so even when they were off in the fields, we thought they were ours to shoot. I guess we earned the title of bona fide "jail birds" thinking that way.

It happened on a beautiful Sunday, with a crisp breeze blowing and the smell of fall in the air. The grain was cut and the pheasants were in the stubble fields. We decided to go to each of our farms to shoot pheasants. We ended up with some forty pheasants shot with .12 gauge shotguns. We took them home to clean, skin, and gut. Pheasant is good eating—loved them then and still do now.

After we finished, we decided to go out and get some more pheasant, so we drove down a dusty back road, further from home. It was Sunday, and we didn't think the game warden would be working. Wrong!

We didn't normally shoot the hens, but a pheasant flew up from where we were standing alongside the road, and one of my buddies shot it. Not good—it was a hen!

We were getting back in the car, and just about that time our "lookout" saw a car coming. We wanted to take off, but the car wouldn't start—the battery was dead. We tried pushing it, but got nowhere. The oncoming car stopped and a game warden stepped out. We didn't know him—he didn't know us either. We had so many guns it looked like we were going to war. Five guys, about eight guns, and besides that, it wasn't pheasant season, *and* we also had that pheasant hen tucked away in the trunk on top of the others. We silently stared at him as he walked up.

The game warden looked at us suspiciously and asked, "What are you boys doing?" Can't remember what all we said, but mostly, "just out goofing around, shooting and stuff."

He said, "Well, can I check your car?" What were supposed to say? "No?"

He discovered the pheasants in the trunk—bad! He hauled us off to his office, where they also had a jail. What we were doing was illegal, we knew it, but in our experience they usually just smacked our hands and took our guns away. Instead, he called our folks.

My buddies dads, and my dad, thought it was funny; maybe a good lesson. They said, "Let them spend a night in jail!" It surprised us that they didn't get us right out because we were the ones that milked the cows and fed the pigs, and did so many chores twice-a-day.

> We weren't too happy about being in jail, but at least we got out of the milking and chores for a day.

When we finally got out, man, we had to write all kinds of papers on fish and game and how to conserve and obey the laws. By then, we didn't feel so smart about what we had done. It was stupid, it really was. We just did it without thinking. Chalk it up as one more lesson learned in growing up. We respected the laws, but we just kind of figured the pheasants were ours to be had, and they weren't, of course. It was against the law. The good part is that we still got to eat the ones we'd cleaned and left at the house!

Lesson Seven: Don't mess with mama—mamas, whether human or animal, have a fierce devoted love for their babies

I learned, *"courage is fear that has said its prayers."*
—Ruth Fishel

Once at the rodeo Rich and I tried to ride a buffalo—we had one chance. We were under the illusion they were slow and docile. Hmmm . . . You guessed it; we never tried to ride one again. But when my dad wasn't home, we sometimes tried to ride the boar pig. On a farm, there is only one boar, because if we had two nobody would survive!

45

We would coerce him into the chute where we branded cattle, and put a saddle on him. Billy was the best at riding him. We would run with pitchforks beside him, to keep the boar away when he got bucked off. I imagine we looked pretty stupid. (Dad broke his tusks out because he would rip apart the other pigs, so that helped us some when we tried to ride him.)

We had two-hundred-fifty acres on the original home farm, and we raised brood sows (female pigs). Hog wire kept them within our acres of land. The sows and little piglets had pens, but when they were loose, sometimes they would go off to have their babies before we got them back into the pens.

My dad could tell when they were close to having their babies, and he would run them into the pens. He wanted them close to the barn where we could watch over them, instead of nesting in a den out on the property. We had a hard time finding sows and their babies if they hid out in the brush or haystacks. My dad always had them counted, and the point of this story is about the time he discovered one was missing.

We knew that she was out there hiding in one of the fields to have her piglets, and we also knew she could be dangerous! Sows are really protective; much like mother bears. They could take your leg off! They have huge mouths (44 teeth), and they can run a seven-minute mile! It's true, and they also have a great sense of smell in their powerful snout. With eyes on the sides of their head, they have a great field of vision. Domestic pigs are rarely aggressive, *except* when they are with their young litter.

Well, everything that happened on the farm makes a great story, and more often a life lesson. I was in the seventh grade when dad sent me down to look for one of these missing sows that he knew had her babies tucked safely away on the property. A hairy job, but somebody had to do it.

My younger brother, Duane, (about six years old) and his friend went with me to look for her. I grabbed the bull whip to protect us. I knew it was dangerous to mess with mama! We wandered around looking for her searching the typical hiding places. We checked the ditches, and the hay stack where winter feed was stowed. Sows sometimes made nests or holes in haystacks that were twenty to thirty feet high. These were great places to have their piglets safely tucked away in the straw.

Duane and his friend ran ahead of me. I yelled at them, "Don't go near that stack!" They were one hundred yards ahead of me. I knew that if that sow was in there and they ran up to the stack, they would be in trouble. I started running and I kept yelling at them, "Don't go up to the stack!" They weren't paying any attention to me. All of a sudden, I heard a growly "Woof!" sound like a bear . . . that big sow came right after them! It was a good thing I took off running towards them when I did.

The boys ran back around that stack, fear etched on their faces, as the mama sow chased right at their heels. They were in big trouble and I started running as fast and hard as I could—I still thank God that I was a fast runner on that day. She came tearing after them so fast. I could see they were running for all they were worth, and all the while screaming as loud as they could—they were scared to death. (Wish I had a picture of the look on their faces!)

She overtook them, running right over the top of them both, knocking them down! I can see it today. She turned around with fierce aggression.

> This mama was ready and able to take a chunk out, or even rip a leg off.

Breathing hard, (like her) I got there just in time, and raised the bull whip, and with one flip of the whip, I stung her snout, changing her mind just as she turned to bite Duane. Man-o-man, I was just in time! If I had been a couple of seconds later, it would not have been a pretty site, or a story I would want to tell.

We went back and got the tractor and wagon. We used it to try to distract the sow away from her piglets, as we ran into the haystack, getting one little piglet at a time. Carrying each one like a football, with *real live pigskins*, we'd run and jump into the wagon. The mama sow watched us like a hawk and tried to get us every time, but once we scored all of her piglets, and had them in the wagon (good training for football), we relaxed some. As we headed in with them squealing away for their mother, she followed us back to where we put them in the pen. She was happy, we were happy!

Though smaller, a sow is as fierce as a mother bear. I never forgot that experience, nor how she sounded and the intensity of having such a close call with that mama sow—and my brother and his friend didn't forget it either!

After I moved to Alaska, I missed the times on the farm. But as far as learning not to mess with mamas, the same is true every time I step into the Alaska wilderness—bears, moose, you name it! Nothing quite like an animal's instincts to protect their young—and I respect that, for their sake *and* mine!

Lesson Eight: Electricity—shouldn't be messed with. There's much more to it than meets the eye

> **I learned,** *"life is a series of experiences, each one of which makes us bigger, even though sometimes it is hard to realize this."*—Henry Ford

We've heard what doesn't kill you makes you stronger. In high school, I went on dates on horseback. Nothing hard about that, but what happened on a horse date once nearly killed me.

My favorite horse, Geronimo, was a huge gelding that had to be at least 2000 pounds and nineteen to twenty-one hands tall. Sometimes things do seem bigger when we're kids, but he was incredibly big, powerful and beautiful. He followed me around like a big dog; he would come when I whistled. I could barely reach his withers; he was at least seven feet tall and extremely fast. We didn't have a fence or corral that could hold him in. He went over them all with confidence and ease, and I loved being on him when he did that! He would nip me to make me hurry or pay attention to him! I had teeth marks from his tantrums. Even so, I still thought of him as my best friend.

One day, my favorite girlfriend back then, Nita, and her horse Zigzag, were riding beside me along the railroad tracks, out on the remote Badlands of Montana. The railroad was between our place and the bison range. We would ride for miles along the road that ran next to the railroad tracks. The freight train didn't come by very often, so it felt like we were the only people in the world when we were out there.

Nita was on her smaller horse and I was on Geronimo, looking down on her. We would challenge each other, "My horse can do this; my horse can do that; I can do this or that!" We talked and rode along, having a great time. Nita had a saddle on her horse, and I was riding Geronimo bare back. After riding for several hours, I was sweaty, Geronimo was sweaty, and the grass beneath our horse's hooves was wet from an earlier rain.

The utility lines and power poles ran alongside the railroad tracks. For some reason, I got a bright idea, or should I say a hair-brained idea, and said to Nita, "I have heard that if you grab the telephone wires and snap them together, it will make a telephone ring somewhere."

I had no clue they weren't telephone wires, but instead high voltage wires! The poles were a long ways apart and the lines weren't high; they sagged in-between. I thought I would just grab the wire and snap two wires together. I did it, and immediately electricity coursed through my body. It felt like someone had hit me on the shoulders with a sledge hammer! I was frozen to that electric wire! The electrical voltage struck so hard that it knocked Geronimo to his knees. (He had steel shoes on front feet only—not on back feet.) The electrical current had gone through me, and then through him and down to the ground! I could not let go of that wire—and I was in extreme pain! I'm so thankful Geronimo was a strong fighter, because I was stuck like glue.

In what must have been just an instant, I could feel every muscle in Geronimo's body ripple, as he got to his feet, taking off like greased lightning! I was torn right off the line when Geronimo bolted. Thank goodness! I know that I would have died if Geronimo had not risen up from his knees and run. No question, he saved my life when he tore me off that power line!

> What was I thinking to do such a stupid thing? Not much!

Nita jumped off her horse to see if I was okay—I wasn't burned and neither was Geronimo. We had many electric fences on the farm and experienced lots of shocks, but nothing ever like that. I was glad to be alive. I chalked that up to choosing to do something stupid as a kid that served no purpose. Only God knows for sure—and all I know for sure is that he was protecting me even when I didn't know it.

Lesson Nine: Water—it was, and is, a precious commodity, but could also get me into trouble.

I learned to, *"Forget past mistakes. Forget failures. Forget everything except what you're going to do now and do it."*—William Durant

When I was in the fifth grade, through junior high school, I had to irrigate and keep the soil wet until the crops began to germinate and grow. I slept in the fields on the ground with the sprinkler pump (not a fun companion), because we had to change the pipes every four hours day and night, all summer long. It was an exhausting 24-hour-a-day job. Food for each day was brought out to me in a paper bag. The only time that I got to come in from the field was on Sunday. I would take a bath, put on clean church clothes, and we all went to church. I was getting so I really liked going since it meant I could come in out of the fields!

Keeping the sprinkler pump running and the pipes changed was a never ending cycle. One part of the job was to move about a mile of pipe—my brothers helped with changing the pipes. As soon as we got the pipes set up and running with water, we had to let them settle down in the ground, otherwise they would tip over. The sprinklers on the top of the pipe were about three feet tall. As they began to pump and turn they would jerk; the water shifted the weight.

Sometimes, I was so tired, as soon as we got the pipes all set up and got them all pumping and turning, everybody would leave, and I would take a nap. But my job was to watch the pipe to make sure the lines stayed upright. A couple of times the lines fell over, and those powerful sprinklers, with so much water pressure, would blow a hole in the ground ten to fifteen feet deep. One particular time that happened when I was so tired I had fallen asleep, but something woke me up! There was about a quarter of a mile of pipe lying down that had blown big holes in the ground wherever there were sprinklers.

I was in a total flap! I got that section of pipe stood back upright, and it was about time to change it again. The other rows that had stayed up were wet like they were supposed to be. My dad sometimes drove out there to check and see how things were going, and unfortunately he happened to come this time. Even though the overturned pipes were now upright, the ground was dry, except for the deep holes of water that the overturned sprinklers had created. From the surface they looked like shallow puddles.

My dad stuck the shovel in the ground and he couldn't figure out why it was dry. He walked along, right over to one of those puddles, and not thinking, he stepped in it, and disappeared! All I could see was his hat floating on the top of the puddle as he went clear down to the bottom of the hole. I knew he knew instantly what had happened—I had fallen asleep and let the line fall over. I didn't even think he could have drowned in that hole! One thing I knew for sure, he wouldn't think it was funny, so I took off running for the other end of the field! I wasn't about to be there when he climbed out of that hole. He got out and left, and wasn't happy with me, but thankfully he didn't run after me. *I survived.* I definitely learned the importance of staying awake on my job with the water sprinklers!

Lesson Ten: Neighbors help neighbors—make it a way of life no matter where you live

> **I learned,** *"Never worry about numbers. Help one person at a time, and always start with the person nearest you."*—Mother Teresa

The only thing needed for evil to triumph is for good people to do nothing . . . is a saying that is often in my mind in so many life situations. I have a habit in life of at least doing something; it makes me feel much better. Sometimes it means I need to apologize to a neighbor, and other times I need to pray for a neighbor, and yet at other times it means that I need to be willing to step up and help a neighbor in my community when they are in a tough place, or going through a rough patch.

Over the years growing up, I watched my dad and neighboring farmers use some of Dad's machinery (like the thrashing machine), and work together to accomplish the hard, ongoing tasks that had to be done in a farming community. I've always tried to do the same for my neighbors in Haines, Alaska.

In Montana, I remember one hot summer day, working away with the other neighbors to put up the hay, how fast it got done. Looking back on it, as we shared machinery and labor, we built strong camaraderie, a healthy community and lifelong friendships. As a kid how everyone worked together impressed me. The women would bring their baked goods, and cook up mouth-watering lunches and dinners for the hay crew. Lots of scrumptious food impressed me, too! Neighbors bring together the best of what each person has to offer, and it makes the world a better place.

A man is a fool to trust himself, but those that use God's wisdom are safe.—Proverbs: 28:26

Neighbors literally save lives sometimes. Laurence saved my brother Duane, who is six years younger than me. With pole climbers, Duane climbed up a telephone pole to get to a nest, his arms around a pole some forty feet up. The wire (30,000 volts) that ran in-between touched him. Laurence, being the great neighbor he was ran over to help when Duane was so critically hurt in this accident.

It was touch and go for Duane, and where he wore his wrist watch burnt clear through his wrist. He lost his hand and wore a hook the rest of his life. The accident changed him forever, in many ways, but it didn't stop him.

I'll never forget Laurence Driscoll's aid to Duane that day. It is one of many stories of our way of life in the country. Neighbors helping neighbors—I see it as human opportunity to offer a helping hand during the ordinary *and* when there is a calamity!

Lesson Eleven: Righteous Anger—Why didn't I help more?

> **I learned,** *"Anyone can become angry. That is easy. But to be angry with the right person, to the right degree, at the right time, for the right purpose and in the right way . . . that is not easy."*—Aristotle

Jesus used righteous anger in the temple, driving out those who bought and sold there, overturning tables of the money changers . . . (Matt. 21:12). His example confirms to us that there are times when displays of anger are necessary and good. But as a mere man I found it is easy to get physically out of control with anger, but with more maturity I learned to depend on God's guidance. I learned to let him be in control of how I handled a head-on situation, rather than me going off half-cocked.

In our farming community, most of us farm boys were kind of cocky, because we were stronger than the kids that lived in town. I admit we did sometimes get into fights, like most boys do, but I always tried to help the underdog when I could, and protect myself when I had to.

As far back as I can remember I always wanted to help people physically, because I can. From the days on the farm through some of the crazy incidents on the ship in the Navy, whether young or old, there is a pecking order among men—some guys just aren't wired for fighting when they need to, or for lack of a better word, macho enough to take care of themselves. That's just the way it is.

Groups of guys can come after one man like a wolf pack. I can think of just such a time on the Navy ship when a guy being picked on and targeted *turned lose the wolf in me* towards the guys that were attacking him. I didn't hesitate, and yelled "One at a time, or both, I don't care!"

I admit that I had it in me to go clear off the end of the charts (so angry that it scared me) with what I feel to this day was "righteous anger," but still anger that needed to be controlled and kept in check. Many times, I feel the Lord restrained me, and brought me sanity when I needed it. Other times, later in my life, I kneeled down in prayer before I intervened (if it was preplanned confrontation), and got right back on my knees to thank God after a volatile event ended peacefully.

God will provide the calm at the exact time we need it, but we have to ask, and be willing to be obedient and follow his guidance. I'm not a boxer, and I've been beat boxing, but turned right around and beat the same guy in street fighting. It's not my claim to fame or anything, but the point is that God watched over me, saved me from the anger that could rise up within me—saved me from making big mistakes with foes on this earth, and protected me from the spirit of the enemy that could use my anger for wrong. One thing I know for sure is God is in charge, and a long, long time ago I willingly placed my anger in his hands to do with it as he wished.

Believe me I *do not* have a Superman complex. Plenty of times, I didn't want to get involved when I saw someone getting singled out and picked on. This was true during all stages of my life. Sometimes I would completely avoid stepping in, but when I didn't help out someone who was defenseless, my conscience suffered for it later, leaving me to mull it over and over: Why *didn't I help? I was there.*

What's the matter with me? I should have done something or said something to stop it!

Anger happens for lots of reasons, and a result of some things we haven't experienced or cannot imagine: A hard home life and neglect, no friends or heroes, competition, a need to belong, male ego, and the list goes on. There are lots of righteous reasons for anger, and as many poor excuses for it, too. I learned *anyone* can be angry, but it needs to be directed at the right person, for the right reason, at the right time, and in the right way.

I'm not sure what the answer is to prevent or help the kids who get into big trouble with anger issues in today's world—the shootings in the schools and public places; kids bullying other kids to the point of being unmerciful; it's terrible! I did get into fights over things like that—some guys just need to be put in their place—to protect what is just and right for the group.

I still think back on times I *could have* and *should have* stepped in to help more in my younger years. It leaves me with a couple of questions. Did it happen that way to prevent me from further problems or maybe even trouble with the law? Or is there still a lesson to be learned for the future? I'm still not completely sure. Oh well, God knows, and he is sure. He will provide the answers when the time is right.

Lesson Twelve: Prayer—the desire to pray began early in me because of my mother

> **I learned**, *"a single grateful thought toward heaven is the most perfect prayer."*—Gotthold Ephraim Lessing

My mother, may God bless her! I know her prayers, saved, saved, saved me! She was the one who prayed in the family, and the one who set a living example of the importance of prayer at meals and other times.

My mom was a very kind, gentle, loving person (though she didn't speak about love)—and I'm so grateful for her, and that she made sure I always went to church, was an altar boy and went to confession. I wasn't quite clear about what to confess, so I didn't exactly make up sins, but I wondered, *what is sin and what is not sin?* I didn't know when I was young. Even so, mom, the nuns and the church set the foundation for my belief in God, and my journey towards eternal life.

My mom wanted my sisters to be nuns, and all of us boys to be priests. Not likely, but then there are always miracles! One brother, Clem, did become a priest. I have pretty much gone to church every Sunday of my life, and if I couldn't find a Catholic Church when I was out-of-town, I would go to a church of another denomination. After all, I know I can worship God in any church that believes in God, Jesus Christ and the Holy Spirit.

Mom, I pray you can hear me in heaven: *Thank you for showing me what it is to be devoted to prayer, for being on your knees before God—for your prayers that covered me and saved me from harm, steered me in the right direction, kept me from disaster or death from all of the dangerous things that happened living and working on the farm. Your prayers pulled me out of a lot of messy situations as I grew older. Thank you!*

I learned a perfect prayer is one that comes from a sincere and loving heart towards God, and has little to do with the words being said perfectly. I still thank God for teaching me that important truth.

I learned dozens upon dozens of things on the farm, but one thing is for sure: farmers are a strong, rare breed, and farming is a challenging and unique way of life that I respect and admire. I was lucky to learn all that I did early on in life, but there's still more I need to learn *now* in life.—Hertz

PRAYER and LIFE LESSONS

"For we are God's fellow workers; you are God's field, you are God's building."—1 Corinthians 3:9

Thank you Lord, Jesus. I am stubborn, sometimes ignorant, and I don't always learn the easy way, but you never give up on me or any of us who call on your name and ask in faith for your help. We are yours to shape and mold for your purpose, your plan. You test us, you refine us like silver, and you bring us to a place of abundance. (Psalm 66:10-12) *Keep your hand upon us. We are yours. Show us the way—your way! Amen.*

PART TWO
IN THE NAVY

Erwin Hertz served in the Navy from 1956-1960

I can imagine no more rewarding a career. And any man who may be asked in this century what he did to make his life worthwhile, I think can respond with a good deal of pride and satisfaction: 'I served in the United States Navy.—John F. Kennedy

I was good to the Navy; the Navy was good to me.—Erwin Hertz

CHAPTER 5

NAVY—MISSOULA TO SAN DIEGO, TO THE SEA AND BACK

The Lord on high is mightier than the noise of
many waters; than the mighty waves of the sea.
—Psalm 93:4

If it'd been an option, I would have tried
with every fiber of my being to become a
Frogman or Navy SEAL.
—Erwin Hertz

Joining the Navy in 1956

I was all set to quit school and go to Alaska, at fifteen years old,
when I was a sophomore in high school. I wanted to go commercial
fishing, with Ted, a friend of mine. I probably would have gone,
but he backed out. I was disappointed, but it was good that I stayed
in school, and finished with decent enough grades to get out of
high school with a degree. *God knew the path I should take, even if
I didn't.*

My senior year, Ted and I skipped school and signed up for
the Navy—we left for boot camp the day after we graduated. We
showed up in Missoula, and they sent twelve recruits off on a train

with some young guy who had military training in high school. He was supposed to get us to basic training camp in San Diego. A far cry from Charlo, Montana! It was high time for me to get away from the farm and grow up.

Growing up also meant recognizing my anger that smoldered just beneath the surface. Was it caused by feelings of insignificance at home? Wanting to marry my girl, but needing to go in the Navy instead? Or was it merely from the compulsion I felt to protect the underdog? Probably all of the above contributed to my anger, but I've always known I wasn't the easy going guy people saw at first glance. I suppose my so-called "righteous anger" benefitted others plenty of times, and served purposes of survival and protection for me at other times, but there is no question that I also walked a fine line of "sanity" with explosive anger. I am thankful to God for watching over me when I was stupid. After the dust settles, we all need to ask—does our anger *solve* problems, or is our anger *part* of the problem?

On the day I left, I got up like usual, did the milking, then came back in and changed my clothes and grabbed my ditty bag I'd packed in my bedroom. I went downstairs and Dad said, "Where are you going?"

All I said was, "I joined the Navy." His response, "Well you could have joined up in the fall when the summer work was done!" I thought he was going to hit me with a chair!

But it worked out okay for my dad and the farm work, because my oldest brother, Richard, was just returning from Army duty in Japan the week I left.

The train trip was exciting since most of us had never been anywhere on a passenger train. The young guy assigned to help us was "green as grass." He was a milk-toast kind of guy.

We spent the first night on the train, then changed trains the next morning. There were two trains parked side by side, and somehow, he got us on the train that was going back to Missoula. We rode along until they checked our tickets. We were down the road quite a ways when the conductor came by to look at our tickets, and he said, "You are on the wrong train!"

That milk-toast kid was really upset! We got off the train, spent the night somewhere in Nevada, and eventually caught another train to San Diego. Overall, it took us a week to get from Missoula to San Diego.

Boot Camp and Electrical School

In boot camp, they asked, "What do you want to do for a job, a career?" I wished I could have been a Frogman or a SEAL. I would have tried to be something like that with every fiber of my being!

But since they were hard up for electricians, and I had seen all the electrical work my dad had done over the years, I opted in for that instead. It wasn't intense or exciting like being a SEAL, but it was an important job, and it proved to be a great career for the rest of my life.

I was all set to go to electrical school, but panicked a bit when they said, "You have to pass a test before you get into the school!" I said, "Oh man!" I didn't have a good history with school and tests, but I passed and made it. God was on my side, even when I didn't know it!

God put good people in my life—I started to recognize it in more ways than one!

Navy Electrical School, in San Diego, had 38 guys in it, and at the end, only 17 passed. I took two years of school in six months, taken along with other Navy classes. Talk about a pressure cooker, especially for a kid like me who wasn't much of a student. I knew I had to have a certain amount of math smarts because they didn't let just everyone in that class, but still, *I was really sweating it!*

None of us in the class knew each other, and I met this Asian guy, Ruffo, from Guam. I liked him right away; he was a great guy. For several days, while we were waiting for our class to start, this big bully kept picking on Ruffo, pushing him around—he was twice his size. I'll never forget the hateful smirk on that guys face as he said and did things to intimidate him. I stepped in to help. The guy wouldn't stop, so I stopped it for him—one punch and it was done. After I smacked him, he wouldn't get up. He caved in too soon, I wanted to hit him again—I wanted to punish him and make him hurt and sweat. I wanted justice for Ruffo, but I kept my anger in check.

The guy kept giving me his most hateful, threatening glare, every time we were in class, trying to make me shrink back. I had ruined his game; he knew he couldn't touch Ruffo if I was around. His parents were there visiting the next weekend. I'd love to have heard how he explained that black eye; a real shiner! Ruffo didn't have trouble with him again.

Even on the day we graduated, this guy kept trying to intimidate me. He said, "I hope I get in a duty station where I'm over you!" I snapped back with, "I'll punch you again—only I'll do a better job next time!"

After that, Ruffo was always there for me, like I was for him; he encouraged and tutored me. One week we had electrical tests about motors, and the hardest motor was a 3-phase motor; all the internal electrical connections inside that motor; single phase and a 3-phase—and obviously the 3-phase was much more complicated. Ruffo grilled me all week before the test—again and again about that 3-phase hookup inside the motor, internal hookups and hookups from the power, and on and on.

> Ruffo had prepared me so well for the test that it almost seemed easy!

I sat right down and wrote a perfect hookup for a 3-phase motor. I missed the test question, (we had different teachers for each phase), and he called me up and said, "You did this 3-phase motor perfect, but the question was for a single-phase motor!" *Heck.*

Ruffo had me studying so much to pass that test that I sat down and drew a 3-phase hookup; I left that teacher scratching his head! I'm so happy to publicly thank, Ruffo again for all that he did for me during our time together in electrical school. Our picture together from those years still hangs in my hallway. Ruffo was a great guy that I know God put in my life for a reason. I wouldn't be an electrician today if it hadn't been for him. The only thing I'm sorry about is that I never saw him again—I wish I could thank him, in person, just one more time.

As I graduated from electrical school and went on, later aboard ship, taking tests always came back to haunt me—but to get a rate I had to pass a test. I'm eternally thankful that God put even more people in my life to help me study and learn; one was an electrical engineer. He helped me pass the electrical engineering course in electrical wiring that I took from the University of Wisconsin.

We had special radio equipment on the ship, and this instructor taught us how to do all the wiring for it and the generators. I worked with him, and liked how he worked with me. He would see me carrying all these books around, and ask, "What are you studying?"

I told him and he said, "Great!" He was an electrical engineer. "I can help you. I'll take a look at your tests before you send them in."

I had to send in at least two lessons a week. He took the time to go over my tests, questions and answers; he would say, "If I were you, I would check some of those answers!" He never told me the ones to check, but I would go over it, and do the whole thing over again. I found lots of my mistakes, and gained confidence each time I passed. I needed to do this well because I really wanted to go through my four years in the Navy and come out with a profession. He taught me several things: how to actually study; have more confidence in my ability; he showed me how words do encourage a person to try to improve and become better at something. (Generous, affirming words weren't something I had experienced growing up.)

The Navy gave me a great education—I became an electrician, a "snipe" on the ship—I had a knack for it, and they offered me more opportunity to go to school after my four years, but I wanted to get out. I had received good electrical training and classes through the Navy, and I got an A—in the two-year course from the University of Wisconsin in electrical wiring and engineering (finished in 13 months). My teachers in high school would have seen those grades they would have hit me in the head! (Chuckle) I studied in the Navy because I did not have a choice!

The Navy was good to me, and I was good to the Navy. I had the discipline it took to get the work on the farm done every day. I did the same on the ship—the work ethic was ingrained.

I didn't experience war action, but we were set and ready, anchored outside of Beruit for a couple of months, but the crisis blew over. Since the Navy anticipated battle, doctors were brought aboard. They didn't have much to do, so they did medical procedures on the guys on the ship, some of them interesting, but not stories to be told here!

Being a Montana farm boy, being confined in a steel box floating around the sea felt like a jail at times

I needed to be on land, but I admit the storms out at sea made me feel alive and heightened all my senses. Those years were a great experience; nothing about the Navy was drudgery since I was always learning. I liked the electrical work—in fact, it was lots easier physically than the work I had done on the farm, so not a problem. After all, I didn't have to milk cows and the food was plenty, and even pretty good food at that. When the city guys would complain about hard work, I'd laugh and say, "You guys don't have a clue!"

Including time in school in San Diego, I was in the Navy for four years. There were plenty of times in the Navy that I saw firsthand how God watches over fools and drunkards—I remember *me being one* of them during a New Year's Eve party in Naples.

This particular New Years, the Navy rented a big ball room with a dining area. The cooks came in from the ship, and we ordered from a menu whatever we wanted. Real dining and dancing, and a live band that wasn't all that great, but it didn't matter; it ended up to be a big blow out. Before long it got so rowdy, the guys in the band left, the guys with their wives went home. The crew took over the instruments and played whatever they wanted. Imagine sailors gone wild!

They were like orangutans, the kind of guys who would do anything, go anywhere, bothered by nothing, no holds barred; *and* also the type of guys who stood by their friends. The crew began racing up and down the hallways on the drink carts, as if they were skate boards, waiters chasing behind yelling in Italian. *Crazy!*

The next morning, I was surprised to find myself way up on the thirteenth floor. I had slept in a narrow, four foot flower box outside the window—who knows how I got there! I didn't budge as I looked down. The people on the sidewalk looked like ants! *Where am I?*

Like I say, God watches over drunkards and fools! I was one that night. I didn't deserve God to watch over me, but I am so thankful he did. God saved me from myself. *This story is one to "write home about"—but in reality, when in the service you don't write home about those nights!*

Out of the Navy

At the same time I was in the Navy, my buddy from home, Archie, went to college at Montana State University in Bozeman. Shortly our lives would cross paths again.

When I got out in 1961, I flew from Norfolk, Virginia to Lake Charles, LA on a DC-6. On my way back home, I stopped to spend some time with my good Navy buddy, Fred Picard, a Creole who lived in Louisiana.

Fred's dad was cut from the same cloth as my dad, so maybe Fred and I were too. He was pretty tough, a little wild and crazy, and a guy I always wanted on my side. Really a great guy—he read the Bible and that impressed me. I stayed with him, working, until I bought a 58' Chevy for eight hundred dollars cash—a good deal I'd gotten from a friend of his. I had my own wheels and it felt terrific after floating on a ship for four years! We raced around there together, pretty free and easy for a couple months, until I decided to head back to Montana.

Then what? I decided to head down to Denver to work, and meet up with a Navy buddy to see how I measured up boxing in the Golden Gloves program that had begun way back in 1923. It promoted amateur boxing in the United States. Today, Golden Gloves produces the majority of competitors for America's boxing teams. Though short-lived for me, it was a good experience.

I remember doing my best in the ring, and the trainer hollering from the corner, "You're doing good kid; keep it up."

I yelled back, "Well . . . better keep an eye on the ref, because somebody's beating the crap out of me." Soon enough, I realized I wasn't going to be a famous boxer and headed home. I'd given it a try, that's all that mattered!

PRAYER and CHANGE

". . . who have borne witness of your love before the church. If you send them forward on their journey in a manner worthy of God, you will do well, because they went forth for His name's sake . . . 3 John 1:6-7

Help us follow you, Lord, wherever our day takes us. Amen!

CHAPTER 6

NAVY NIGHTMARE: NEVER DOUBT GOD'S PROTECTION

The Lord is my rock and my fortress and my deliverer;
My God, my strength, in whom I will trust; My shield
and the horn of my salvation, my stronghold.
—Psalm 18:2

To this day, I know that God loved me through
this challenge. He's carried me spiritually, mentally and
physically through *many dangers, toils and snares.*
This is just one of 'em.
—Erwin Hertz

Navy, 1959-1960

I got out of the Navy in May of 1960, but a "nightmare" happened shortly before I was discharged. It was a very scary, stressful, out-of-control event. I couldn't control a thing, but trusted and waited on God's timing and justice. I prayed every day, yet some days, God seemed far, far away. *Grace had brought me thus far and grace would bring me home.* I know without a doubt that God protected me spiritually, mentally and physically—only through his protection and grace, and to his glory, did I escape this *trial* and *snare.*

We were aboard ship in Naples, Italy. A new guy came aboard. I'll call him Williams. He joined in our engineering division, as a boiler man as far as I know. When he came aboard, he did not fit in and he didn't care if he did; he didn't want to. Right away I noticed that he was belligerent and had a big chip on his shoulder; it stood out for everybody to see.

Some people like to be on big ships, like aircraft carriers with 5000 people aboard so they can get lost in the crowd. Our ship only had a 180 man crew. On a big ship, a crew member can get away with lots of things, but it's not easy to get lost in the crowd on a small ship. Sometimes rated guys would throw their weight around, there were other conflicts and stuff like that; our ship wasn't perfect, but a small ship is like a small town, and everybody knows what somebody does right, and what somebody does wrong. It goes without saying, we all had to work together and get along in our small space. We needed harmony.

I'll set the stage. Our free time, social time went like this on the ship:

Whether we were in or out of port, after supper, movies were shown on the tank deck where we carried all the trucks, cars, gear and equipment that we needed for maneuvers in the Mediterranean. I wasn't concerned about watching movies all that much, but the duty electrician was in charge of showing it. The movies came from the shore base in Naples. They were not updated or rotated too well, so we saw many of the same movies over and over, but still, gave us some entertainment.

We also had a boxing team aboard the ship. We boxed and wrestled, and it was all very friendly. We needed to keep in shape, stay busy and let off steam. The boxing spars in the evenings helped. We had plenty of room on the tank deck to work out. We'd lift weights, and jump up, grab the "parallel bars" that ran the length of the tank deck—for 350 feet. Hand-over-hand, we would race each other on those bars, to the far end and back. There weren't very many people that could do it, but it was right up my alley. *I could swing like an ape, I guess!* The other guys liked to watch us, and cheer us on as we'd wrestle and box, or race on the bars before the movie—we entertained ourselves and entertained them.

From the get-go it wasn't good with Williams; he was aggressive and spoiling for a fight. When we put mats down, he'd join us, boxing and wrestling. Most of us got to know each other before trying to wrestle, but not him—he was not a sportsman and not interested in being a friend to anyone; he was out for blood!

The rest of us liked the competition and the sport of it, but Williams would deliberately try to hurt people, right off, even as the new guy on the ship. The chip on his shoulder stood for "bully!" He didn't do anything for fun. He was a big, over six feet tall and weighed over two hundred and twenty pounds.

Time went by. We had our movies every night, and the same group of guys went early to box, and to enjoy the other stuff we did. Williams made it stressful for everybody. I don't know why he decided to pick on me—I was only five feet eight inches and 165 pounds. I was in shape and worked out with a body bag and speed bag (but didn't want to end up in the other kind of body bag).

Even though I joined the boxing team on ship, I was not the best boxer. We had some really good boxers; we boxed and wrestled to keep in shape, sharpen our skills, but never to try to hurt each other. Even when I had differences with guys on the ship, I didn't bully or pick on anyone, but got along. But Williams kept picking me out to try to intimidate and dominate during our time "for sport."

He shoved, strong-armed me, and not in a friendly way. I could out-lift other guys, but was still friends with them. Seemed he cared mostly about pushing me around, ramming for a showdown. He kept on and on, and after a while, he got more belligerent and obnoxious. I got sick of it—*I got mad!*

One night, Williams got especially rough. He dogged me, determined to put me down, not gently, but tried to *throw* me down on the deck. He wanted to show everybody he could do it. I knew Jujitsu, jumped rope and always tried to keep my strength up. It was clear he wasn't going to stop until he put me down. *He was definitely too much of a good thing!*

Finally, I'd had enough, and in a split second, I put him down so hard and fast that he didn't know how he got on the floor. He got up, and he was like a mad dog, and red-faced! I was ready for him, whatever he wanted to give me at that point. I was mad, too! He stood up, glared and stomped off. He left the area, and we didn't see him for days!

My first big *clash* with him was a big one, because I know he "lost face." He was trying to make a reputation for himself; not sure for what—being a bully, I guess; I have no idea! I still have no clue why he chose me to push around—maybe because I was smaller than some of the guys. I wasn't the best boxer or wrestler; or maybe it was because I was popular on the ship and I had been there a long time. I don't know.

> I hate bullies; I hate it when anybody picks on someone who can't protect themselves.

A lot of guys don't have a clue about fighting of any kind. They *won't* or *don't* want to fight, and bullies make a point to pick on them—they target those who don't know how to take care of themselves. It's not like I'm ever out to find a fight, but I will stand up for myself when I have to.

As Navy ship's go, we were "small cheese," a small ship. We did maneuvers and war games, and during those times, we had gas trucks and other flammable stuff on the tank deck ready to go out on our maneuvers. We didn't carry the gas trucks onboard unless we were going somewhere, but sometimes the trucks were on deck for days at a time because they were huge trucks full of Avgas, parked in specific areas on the deck; it all took some time to prepare.

Along this time, all this equipment was onboard, and I had fire watch. I had to check all the stations aboard ship at least once an hour; the engine rooms and the generator rooms and different places where there was fuel; like fuel tanks, the boiler room and such spaces. The only person that could be in those spaces at those times was the guy who was on fire watch, a rated man with the authority to be in that space. I was one of those men.

This guy, Williams, hadn't been on the ship that long when we had a fire in the main engine room. Nobody knew how it was started, but we knew it started in the bilges. There was always oil of some kind in the bilges because of leaks from the pipes and tanks.

Kind of unusual where the fire started, in the main engine room—the guys who worked that area kept it really clean. They lived and worked there; it was their home. Everything was in tip-top shape.

But it was a tough fire to get to, which made it harder to put out. I was only involved because I had fire watch duty. The engine rooms were in the bottom of the ship, and the only way to get to them was with ladders that went from the top of the main deck of the ship, clear down to the very bottom of the ship where the engine room was located.

They had a horrible time getting to the fire, and we all knew there wasn't much time to do it. With a fuel fire, it starts heating up the decks above it, below it and around it. Obviously it melts and catches other things on fire as it heats up! There is nothing worse than a diesel oil fire or a gas fire aboard ship. We carried gas in fuel tanks for the airplanes.

They fought to get this fire out—worked on it for a couple hours. Everything was black; and I mean everything; really black from the smoke, but it finally was put out! A fire in the "steel box" of a ship is like heating up a frying pan.

They got the engine room all cleaned up; they had to paint it and get everything "spick and span" again. That was no small job. The guys were proud of that place, and took pride in keeping it safe and spotless, to avoid problems, or the possibility of catching fire.

We all speculated how the fire might have started, but decided it must have been an accident. They thought somebody might have thrown something in the bilges accidently because it was the fuel in there that caught on fire. In the meantime, Williams was always around—still with a chip on his shoulder. The whole "losing face" incident with me stuck in his craw, I guess.

Mess Hall—Mess!

One day, I was going through the mess line and Williams was there. He stayed away from me since the *incident.* The boiler room (heated all the water for the ship) was right below the mess deck. Sometimes I would see him standing there when he was on duty. Guys that had boiler watch would come up to the top of the ladder, talk to somebody, and then go back down on watch in the boiler room.

I didn't want to make an enemy or be at odds with anybody, but sometimes it couldn't be avoided. Some people didn't get alone with anyone, and on our ship, that was Williams. I was going through the chow line and Williams was standing up at the top of the boiler room ladder. The mess cooks put the food on our trays. Some things we could have seconds, unless it was steak or lobster!

I made my way through the chow line and as I got down to the end, Williams was standing back where the cooks stood. He grabbed a can of red hot pepper, reached over and dumped it all over my tray. I hadn't talked to Williams or done anything since putting him down on the mat, but right then he made it clear he held a grudge! I could not believe he did this, and I went into instant mad! I am not an angry person by nature, *but that was my supper!*

I am sure they would have given me more food, but that wasn't the point, he singled me out. The whole mess deck was full of men. I stepped towards him, didn't pause; just slammed the tray right in his face. I slammed it hard, and all that red pepper, and food, was in his face, all over him, running down his front. *Now he really had a red face!*

I don't know what was up with Williams, just that he had it in for me, I guess. Now he really did have something to be mad about. *He started all of it; I didn't!* I don't pick fights. You could have heard a pin drop in that dining hall. Williams left.

Malta and the bombs

Our ship went out on sea maneuvers, sometimes for a month or so, but this time it was a short trip. After coming back, we had to go to Malta (population of around 200,000 people) to move the bombs and ammunition out of the airbase there. They wanted the U.S. Naval airbase to leave their country. It was a little country. As I recall, independent from the British by then. Anyway, it was a small country below Sicily.

We emptied our ship, and went from Naples to Malta which was a short distance. Our tank deck was about 300 feet long and forty or fifty feet up to the deck above the tank deck. Big trucks drove on there all the time—it was about forty or fifty feet wide.

After we got there, we loaded bombs that were from fifty to 2000 pound bombs each. It took us days because it was not your ordinary stuff to pack around. We had munitions on our ship all the time, but not like that. (These were put on deck, above the engine room.)

We stacked bombs for days, very carefully, so they wouldn't move when we were out at sea. Thinking back, I would think more trips might have been better, instead of making such big loads at one time. *We were really loaded up*—a few mistakes and *we could have blown up!*

We got ready to sail this load back to the Naples airbase. I was talking to one of the engine room men in charge; he was from New York. We talked about putting a watch down in the engine room because we had an inkling something was up; we suspected that something bad could happen again. We weren't convinced the earlier fire was an accident, but we couldn't begin to figure out who would set a fire aboard ship! People smoked, but they were very careful about it.

He and I were on the same page. We talked more about it. Having somebody on watch was a good idea. "We should put a watch down here! This is a good time to blow up a ship with all those bombs on board!" But we didn't act on our concerns.

"Fire, Fire, Fire!"

Like most nights, the movie was showing and I was doing my regular fire watch, checking every space, once an hour. I opened the hatch to the main engine room and it was smoking—not again, not now! It was black smoke, fuel driven. I ran down to the quarter deck where everything is directed from aboard ship. There were two guys on watch on the quarter deck with a pistol and a rifle—they got things in motion.

Then I ran down to the movie area and I said, "Fire! Fire! Fire!—fire in the main engine room!" Everybody knew the drill; it had only been a few months since the other one. And there we were, with all those bombs, right above the engine room on the tank deck, on board ship. Man, it was something—and fighting the fire had the same problem as before; they could not get to it because of the thick smoke that came billowing up.

There are ways of flooding an engine room, too, but that is complicated because of all of the electrical components involved in shutting everything down. The main power went through the engine room, and if that filled full of water, not only would we be out of power, other things would be taken out. Oil was pumped to different tanks to keep the ship level. The crew went down with fire hoses to put it out, because of where it was. All of the firefighting had to be done manually, because our ship was built in the late 30's, and we couldn't just close the hatch and turn on a sprinkler system like today. The guys were skilled and efficient, but still the smoke made it tough. It was several hours before everything was secure. Damage control was in charge, and I took my orders from them, did what I was told; that was my job. I headed to the generator room to turn off a bunch of different systems that were electrical.

I had gone from Fireman, to Electrical Apprentice, to II Class Electrician by this time in my Navy career. Man, oh man, did we fight that fire! Since we were still in port in Malta, if the ship blew up the town of Malta would go too. Malta was built on hills, and the main part of town was right at the edge of the sea port. An explosion from the bombs we had on board would have wiped out the town, the whole sea port and most of the island; a scary thought.

The guys fought like crazy and put that fire out, just like they had done before. This time, they were *very* serious about finding out what happened.

I was the prime suspect! The area where it started was restricted space. Anyone who didn't belong there would look like a pink elephant! There were fifteen, or more, of us on quarantine from the engineering division—all were under investigation. We couldn't leave the ship.

> Once the fire was out, right away, I got the bad news.

I had been on the fire watch—the long and short of it, Williams set the fire on my watch because he was trying to sabotage my life and my career. Nobody could be in that space but me. I was not a happy camper—my life was about to explode, but once again as life would have it, I couldn't control or change a thing! I had to trust God the truth would surface. If not, I faced fifty years in prison for sabotage.

I figured he probably lit the fire an hour or so before I found it. There was only two ways to get into the engine room; there was a hatch on each side of the ladder, and the only way to get down there was on the ladder. The other side was rarely ever used even though there was a ladder access and escape hatch there, too. I think that is the one he slinked in to do his dirty work.

In the meantime we went back to Naples and unloaded all the bombs. I was still on the ship; my friends talked to me; other guys were spooked about talking to me because they didn't want to look like they were involved. In the military it felt like I was guilty until proven innocent! When you are a civilian, you are innocent until proven guilty. By that time, I only had less than three months left in the Navy. Shocking, horrible way to go out if my career ended like this!

The Navy sent the FBI and ONI (Officer of Naval Intelligence) onto our ship, and we were on quarantine. Everybody in the engineering division was on quarantine. I was the prime suspect right from the get-go, because I was the only one that could be in that restricted area at that time. It was a very scary and confusing time for me.

They took all of my clothing, all my mail, they took everything that I owned or was in contact with. (fifteen other guys were suspect, and only eight later on). They cut all the seams out and the cuff of my pants to see if there were any hidden messages or anything incriminating. I still did my job aboard ship, but people were looking at me crosswise. I had never been a prime suspect of a crime—it was awful! I was only in my early twenties, and with the stress of this I didn't know which way was up.

A lot of things were involved with the investigation, especially since they thought someone had tried to sabotage the ship to destroy Malta; those bombs blowing up would have wiped it off the map. It wasn't so much about the ship and all of us being blown up; Malta being destroyed would have been an international incident.

I stayed in prayer

I trusted God and just kept doing what I was supposed to do in my job as an electrician. It was really quiet onboard; usually there was always lots of talking and joking going on aboard ship, but not now. This was a very somber and serious time—everyone felt it.

They told me, also, that I had to write down everything that I had done in the past two years. I had to account for all my time day and night; of course that is impossible. They read all my mail that was coming in for me, and all my back mail. They were not very friendly to me. I hadn't done anything, but they didn't know that.

There were eight of us who could go into the engine rooms. They gave all of us lie detector tests. From the get-go, they said that they thought I had something wrong with my heart. I imagine I was a little stressed out; actually big time stressed out! They didn't send me to the doctor or anything; we didn't have a doctor anyway.

They sent some new guys on the ship in the deck force. The deck force is for men who don't fit any place else. They scrape and grind paint off the deck all day and then prime it, and then repeat the same thing further down the ship. All year long that was their job, all around the ship. They had these grinders; and oh man, talk about noise! Suddenly there were two new guys on the deck force; we knew they were plants. They were agents.

It was a time where those of us who were suspect didn't fit in; not because we weren't getting drunk like everybody else, but because we were in big trouble—our whole ship was in trouble until this got resolved!

I took lie detector tests three different times. Of course, they questioned me over and over at different times about different things; where I was, about my family and everything. This went on for a few months. I'd gone from the burning frying pan to the pressure cooker! My time to get out of the Navy was really getting close, but I didn't even think about it. Instead I thought about facing a possible fifty years in jail! They told me that right up front. Every time I was questioned by the FBI, there was somebody watching me to see my reactions. It was very intense; very intense!

Eventually some of the crew began talking to me. I was the same guy and I would always help out and stood my watch and did beyond what I was assigned to do, just like before this horrible nightmare of an event. I was a lot more somber, I will tell you that.

How they finally caught him

As the investigation kept going on, aboard ship, the cross-questioning started turning up some consistent problems that arose at the same time Williams had been assigned to our ship. Things were missing from our racks and lockers, and with more questioning, it was Williams who was always spotted walking around the areas where "stuff" happened. Radio men slept in the radio room, and one man saw Williams go down to the engine room—using the other hatch. The FBI started piecing stories together.

We all had our racks on the ship, and you went and talked to other guys on the ship, but why was it that Williams was always seen in a place where his locker wasn't? The rack was a bed; why would Williams be there if it wasn't his rack? In their cross-questions the pieces began to fall together.

FBI began to question him more intensely, repeatedly. He refused to take a lie detector test. The investigators started questioning the engineering crew again about stolen items. When something was stolen, who was there, did you see anyone walking away, and were they supposed to be there, was it strange for them to be there?

The FBI working on the case were smart and sophisticated people. They knew what they were doing with the investigation—boy, am I ever glad they did. Williams name became the common denominator; he showed up more and more in the answers to their questions.

It looked like Williams was in the loop—I thank God that they really zeroed in on him! Why else would he refuse to take a lie detector test? The tables turned fast after that; they questioned him upside-down, crosswise, sideways, and every-which-way! The investigators checked his complete background; where he was before, his duty stations, problems that he had before he came to our ship. This opened a whole Pandora's Box on him.

Of course we weren't told about Williams then, but come to find out later, they found out that he was trying to sabotage his father's name, his Naval career, for whatever sick reason. His father was a jet pilot on one of the aircraft carriers.

Now, they had to get him off the ship. The crew would have killed him, because every one of *us* would have been killed if he had succeeded and all those bombs would have exploded! They learned he had set other fires before being on our ship? What the heck was the matter with this guy?

Last we heard he was in Germany in prison/mental confinement . . .

Everybody was glad that they got Williams off the ship—fast! He was one guy I sure never wanted to see again, but at the same time, someone I'll never forget.

Right on time—honorable discharge

My life changed really fast and for the best. I found out from the crew how they stood up for me when the FBI questioned them. I helped everybody, worked hard, took classes and studied hard for two years of electrical engineering and electrical wiring aboard ship. I did everything I could for people, even when it wasn't convenient or a job I liked to do. I would stand watch to help somebody out. If someone was afraid to do a certain job that had to do with electrical, I would do it. My solid reputation paid off. I felt the ship was our home, *my home!*

The crew told me later, and it still makes me tearful all these decades later when I talk about it, "Hertz was a great guy." I'm amazed about all the kind, complimentary things they said about the kind of person I was, how hard I worked on the ship, things I'd done for them, my honesty and friendship.

The FBI met with me and sincerely apologized for what they had put me through. They gave me all my personal things back, and told me they were impressed with my Naval record. They talked to me quite awhile, and asked what my plans were now that my four years were up. They said they were honored to know me. They had gotten to know me, better than most, during the investigation. I'm confident that God orchestrated the people who stood by me and the men who worked the case. This prevented me from ever being accused and convicted of such a horrendous criminal act. It was bad enough to be a suspect. I tried to honor God, and I know without a doubt God honored me!

After that, the engineering officer and I met. He and I were close. He kind of laughed and said, "You know I have to give you the "shipping over" talk!"

"Yeah right, I want to 'ship over'." We both laughed, but what I had gone through was so fresh in my mind, I just wanted out! I had great camaraderie with all the guys, and missed many of them, but it was time to move on from the Navy. I did my formal discharge from Norfolk, and the rest is history. I've missed a lot of those guys from the ship over the years—we helped each other. They were good, loyal friends that I will never forget! I've said it before, but I'll say it again, "I was good to the Navy, and the Navy was good to me."

PRAYER and PROTECTION

"But let all who take refuge in you be glad; let them ever sing for joy. Spread your protection over them, that those who love your name may rejoice in you."—Psalm 5:11

Lord, it was amazing how you protected me through all that mess in the Navy. I never have to wonder if you are protecting me now. I am so thankful. I am sold out for you, Lord, lock stock and barrel—I give you praise for everything.

And Lord . . . yeah, okay Lord, I am still listening now! I wouldn't trade this life that you've given me for anything! Amen.

PART THREE

NORTH TO ALASKA

"The Last Frontier"

Erwin Hertz moved to Haines, Alaska in 1961
He lives there today, until when—*only God knows* . . .

The midnight sun, in Alaska, makes me think
of the cross, the key to eternal life!
—Erwin Hertz

CHAPTER 7

NORTH TO ALASKA— DREAMS CAN COME TRUE

You will show me the path of life; in your
presence is fullness of joy; at your right
hand are pleasures forevermore.
—Psalm 16:11

Alaska is exciting, beautiful, wide open country
with job opportunities for young men. It is an
adventurous and less restricted place, with a more
relaxed life style. In 1961, you might say it was
electrifying for me to go to Alaska where there were
jobs and a never-ending wilderness to explore.
—Erwin Hertz

When I got out of the Navy, and my dream of becoming a professional boxer came to a screeching halt, I settled back in at home in Montana. About the same time, my good friend, Archie, was done with college in Bozeman. Archie was going to drive to Alaska with Frank, (a friend on his college wrestling team) who was from there. He asked me, "Why don't you go to Alaska with us?"

I didn't hesitate, and said, "I'd love that!" I had my education and experience from the Navy and I figured I could put it to good use with a job in Alaska. We loaded up two cars of us—me and Archie, and Frank (the friend from college who was from Haines,

Alaska), and two college buddies that were going along with him in his car.

All set, we headed north for Haines, Alaska in June, 1961. We drove up the only way we could—the Alcan Highway, man what a rough and unpredictable trip that was in those days! (The Alcan Highway was constructed during World War II for the purpose of connecting the neighboring U.S. to Alaska through Canada. It begins at the junction of Dawson Creek, British Columbia and runs to Delta Junction, Alaska, via Whitehorse, Yukon. Completed in 1942 at a length of approximately 1,700 miles, as of 2012 it was 1,387 miles long. The difference in distance is due to constant reconstruction of the highway, which has been rerouted and straightened out in numerous sections. The highway was opened to the public in 1948. Legendary over many decades for being a rough, challenging drive, the highway is currently paved over its entire length.)

Seemed like we drove forever—on and on and on! It rained a lot so we slept in the car by the road, and when it was dry we slept in sleeping bags under a tree by the road. Built fires, cooked our food. A great time!

Driving up the Alcan—all 1600 miles of that rough, narrow, beat up road was tough. The nearer we got to Alaska, it was totally unpaved road—pot holes, gravel and dust!

Driving in Canada, we were halfway through the country before we realized that what we reading the road signs as miles per hour, when in fact, they were written in the metric system. We didn't get it—no wonder we barely made it with that mentality. Gas stations were far and few, but worth every stop, because those men in the gas stations could have written a book—crazy stories that totally entertained us.

The extreme dust was suffocating, so people didn't want us to pass them. I remember two ol' gals in a big blue Cadillac that were going so slow, driving in the middle of the road so we would not pass them. *Made me crazy!* With their big car they thought they owned the road—we got so tired of it. They didn't want to eat our dust—can't blame them, but we needed to get by them or we would never get to Alaska.

I kept on their bumper and every time we got to a hill or a big curve, they would pull over in the right lane. It was spooky to try to get by them. Every time they pulled into the right lane it never failed, a big freight truck came from the other way. Always a busy highway since it was the only one.

Finally, the gals had to get in the right lane. It looked clear, so I stepped on the gas of my '58 Chevy and got around them by the skin of my teeth. Frank and the rest were still back there in the dust with those ol' gals. Something happened with Frank's car, and we had to stop, and wouldn't you know those ol' ladies passed us again!

The whole trip probably would have been easier to take on a horse (like Geronimo), especially on the upper end of the road! We had several days of choking dust, ruts and dirt, flat tires, and stops to work on our cars (thankfully Frank was a super mechanic).

I was grateful that we were a self-sufficient creative bunch of young men—we had some interesting problems to solve. We even wrapped a rubber inner-tube around our gas tank because the pounding gravel tore holes in a car's gas tank after days of driving on the upper end of the road. One of the roads had washed out, and a detour went along the railroad tracks. That wasn't fun, but we just kept on, never getting stuck for long. We didn't have AAA or anything like that to give us roadside service, so what choice did we have?

One day we decided we needed to find someplace to take a bath. It was about time! Driving along, Frank stopped so we could jump in a river that was only a couple of feet deep. We couldn't wait to scrub up. We took all of our clothes off and jumped in!

It wasn't that warm, so we didn't plan to be there long, but here we are splashing away in our birthday suits, and as luck would have it, a tour bus comes driving right by us! There we were, naked as jaybirds! What could we do? Nothing! We just stood there. Everybody was smiling and waving, the driver was honking the horn, pointing out the local color—us! We decided they just wanted to *welcome us to Alaska!*

When we got further up to Alaska, closer to the Yukon River, Frank made all of us get out of the car, yelling, "Everybody pee in the Yukon." That is part of the ritual of coming to Alaska.

I said sarcastically, "Oh yeah, right!"

In White Horse, Canada, a pretty good sized town we stopped along a few clothes lines and picked up a few towels and things we needed. Wrong! This huge Malamute came out after us. He didn't look a bit friendly, but seemed to like me okay, so we got out of there without any chunks out of our legs—but still, our conscience should have bothered us. Not sure it did!

Hey Frank, are we in Alaska yet?

We crossed over the border into Alaska, and Frank took us to Klukwan, an Indian settlement. He told us that Klukwan was Haines. Klukwan was a primitive, small village, with older houses that were badly in need of repair, back in 1961.

We looked at each other, took a deep breath, pulled up to a vacant lot and started unloading our cars right alongside the road. We figured that was where we going to stay. He broke out laughing at the joke he was playing on us. We all jumped on him; I was a "fly weight" in comparison. He was a big wrestler kind of guy. We were young men, and you know how it is, boys will be boys!

Once we finally figured out Klukwan was not Haines, but that it was forty miles north, we got back into the car and drove onto Haines, stopping first at Mosquito Lake to wash the mud and dirt that was caked on the car *and us!*

Just outside Haines, Frank had a little cabin that he had built when he was in high school; all five of us stayed there. He had a few dishes, and the first night we made a fire and cooked up some dinner, all so excited.

After dinner, I asked, "Where's the water?" Frank said, "Mud Bay is right down below us."

Archie and I took dishes down to wash, but the tide was out. Only mud—we couldn't believe that the water had all but disappeared. There was a lot of water when we had arrived earlier—what happened? Tides flowed in and out in channels in Alaska, too? Duh?

In those days there was no hunting season, no tags, or at least nobody paid attention to it much. Frank had all the guns we needed, and we walked high up on the mountain to get goats. First time, we got two—some easy good eating.

We got acquainted at the town dances; everyone had a good time. Booze was a way of life in Haines. I didn't mind having a few beers, but I couldn't keep up, and even as a young man didn't like to drink that much. In small-town Alaska, in the 1960's, every night was Saturday night. One weekend, they had a shooting. I thought I'd seen a few things, but said, "Man, this is just like the old west!" Welcome to Alaska! It was, and to this day is a great place to live—and a matchless life journey of interesting people, experiences and places.

Jobs—small to big

I tried getting a job at the saw mill in Haines, but there were more people than jobs, even with only about 400 people in the Haines area. After the fourth of July activities were over, we all split up and got serious about looking for work. Frank was a logger and he went to Sitka and he took his two buddies with him.

Archie and I went to Skagway since they needed people to work on the railroad. We flew the twenty miles to Skagway, across the channel, since there wasn't a road. Today it takes less than two hours traveling there by ferry on the Alaska Marine Highway.

I worked there for a couple of years. The first summer, I worked on the bridge gang, up at White Pass building a snow shed. The snow shed (thirty feet high, forty feet long) was built so the train could get through the pass in the winter. It sat on the track with doors that opened at both ends when the train went through. It was typical to have thirty feet of snow, or sometimes more in the winter.

It was summertime when we began, and wow, was the wind ever blowing. It was raining and cold in the summer on the pass. I didn't expect that! The seasoned workers said the only way to stay warm up here in the summer was to wear black wool underwear. Somebody gave me a pair and I wore that underwear working in the rain. It kept me warm even though I just wore regular clothes over it.

I liked the work. We had to dig down and put creosote block for the foundation. 12x12 beams were used to construct a snow shed that could withstand all the heavy snow, protect the railroad tracks, and keep the trains running over White Pass throughout the winter. We lived in railroad cars, right there in White Pass; they were placed there for workers to live in.

It was an interesting and good job, and we sure saved our money since we were in the middle of nowhere. We earned three dollars an hour on the American side and the Canadians were only getting one fifty an hour. They worked on the track changing ties; we were on the bridge gang. We all ate in a mess hall, and all of us, the Canadians and Americans became good friends. It was a bit tricky up there, because we were getting different wages, but they were great guys to work with. We worked there all that summer and got the snow shed built.

When the summer was over, Archie joined the Air Force, so he headed back to the lower 48. I went back to Skagway and began working at the Glacier Section, out of town with an Eskimo, named Takjack. We did track patrol there. There was another guy that took care of the station. It was slow in the winter, but we had our hands full keeping the tracks clear of the rocks that fell down the mountain. We had to do track patrol every morning. It was way out in the boonies, wild country, but like all the other things about Alaska, I thought it was amazing working there.

Come September, Takjack and I were changing ties on the railroad one day. Watching up the mountain, we spotted a herd of mountain goats way, way up high.

I said, "I wonder if we could go up after work and get one?" He just looked at me.

I asked him, "You want to go?" and Takjack said, "Sure!" We went back and told the guy that we were going goat hunting.

He said, "That is a long ways! It's a lot farther than it looks!"

I felt confident, "I know, but I have the right shoes." We started up the mountain and it was a light rain. As we hiked up, thankfully, I was in a lot better shape by this time in the summer to do a heavy-duty mountain hike.

Takjack kept slowing down. I stopped and asked him, "Why don't you build a fire and just stay here, and I'll go up and get us a goat and come back. Since it gets dark early, I'll see you by the fire light when I come back down. Takjack stayed there. He was nipping on something in his bottle. I didn't say anything, just asked him to keep the fire going.

I hiked and hiked. It was getting twilight and I spotted a herd of goats in a high meadow. I walked out; they just looked at me and kept eating. Even though they were wild goats, they didn't care one bit about me. I walked right up to one, grabbed a hold of his horn, and he just looked at me, chewing away, with not a care in the world. I realized that I couldn't shoot one since I couldn't get him back down the mountain—in the dark of the night, anyway.

I just put my gun over my shoulder; I had a sling on it across my chest; I started down, and needed to go fast because it was getting dark. Not even a moon, and in September it gets pitch dark at night, unlike summertime.

In trouble

I finally came out on the face of the mountain and I could see Takjak's fire. It was a long ways down; just a little speck; *way down there!* I got serious about getting down the mountain, but I made a huge mistake. Praise be to God I am still alive! I took off down through the trees, running and jumping over the terrain, and it got steep—then all of a sudden I started falling. I had stepped over what seemed like a cliff . . . nothing beneath me! I was falling . . .

And of all things, I realized it was what a mountain climber calls a "shoot" where the rocks go up straight and there's like a hollow channel in-between them. I fell down, not sure how far, and my rifle got stuck sideways. There I was hanging, by my rifle—dangling from my rifle sling, in the shoot of the mountain. It was pitch black!

I touched one side then I realized I could touch the other side with my foot. Both ends of my rifle barrel gouged into the rock; one end had rubber on the butt end (put on there to protect my shoulder from the kick) of the gun. My rifle wedged in, stayed and stuck there.

I decided the best thing to do was to turn around in the sling and get my feet on one side and my hands on the other. Just like crawling up between two walls, I climbed down the shoot—one slip and I would not be here talking to you today! It shook me up—I prayed all the way down.

I finally got safely down to the bottom. I couldn't believe it when I looked back up. I couldn't see a thing; it was pitch black. The rest of the hike down I didn't let go of one tree limb until I got a hold of another one. I made it down to Takjak, and told him what happened. It was well into the morning when we got back to the workplace. I still remember that goat trip and what could have been. As always, God was faithful, as he has been with every fall, and every *uneven* step of my life!

Skagway, snow storm, train, and . . . Layton Bennett, bush pilot

It was wintertime and I was in Skagway working on the dock for the railroad. A huge snow slide barreled down on and around the front and back of the train locomotive, trapping the engine and its crew up on the mountainside. A rescue had to get the train engine back in to town before it froze up. In the meantime, the crew was up there shoveling coal in the boiler to keep the engine fired up. The railroad needed to get a cat skinner in from Haines who could get up the track, and to them, and plow them out. It was too dangerous, and there was no one in Skagway that would do it. They asked me if I knew anybody that was a cat skinner, and I said, "Yeah, I do." Actually it was Frank.

The logging camp in Sitka had shut down, so Frank was back working in Haines. They were really in a flap to get the train down the mountain. They needed someone right away.

They asked, "Can you call him and ask him if he would come over and take a D-6 Cat up to plow the slide away from the train? We must get it, and the crew, back down the mountain?"

I called Frank and told him what they needed, but also told him, "It is going to be really dangerous. The only way that you can get up there is to take the cat on the railroad tracks. It will be steel on steel—the cat track on the railroad track. You could slide over into the canyon in a split second!"

Frank said, "Yeah, I will go ahead and come over. I'll come take a look."

Layton Bennett, the best bush pilot around, agreed to fly him over, even though the seventy mile-an-hour winds weren't letting up anytime soon. Even if the wind got worse, it wouldn't deter Layton. As a WW II veteran pilot—he'd done it all.

Frank had directions for us. "Layton said that you have to have about ten guys to grab the plane when he sets it down, or it will flip right over in the wind."

I assured him that I would have people waiting for the plane. I talked to some people in Skagway and I cleaned out some bars to get enough men. (Not hard to find plenty of men in bars in Skagway, Alaska.)

We were all ready and waiting at the landing strip. The wind was roaring. Skagway is like a big funnel that the wind whips through—not much snow stays on the ground there because the wind literally blows it away.

We waited at the airport, getting ready to grab the airplane and sure enough, here came Layton, flying over the airport—he just kept the plane in flying mode—putting it down more like a helicopter. As soon as the plane landed, we grabbed it; we held it to keep it from being picked up by the wind.

Frank and Father Miller got out, as Layton prepared to fly right back. I asked Frank, "How was the trip?" He kind of laughed nervously and said, "I knew that the Lord didn't care about me and Layton, so if it hadn't been for Father Miller being with us, we wouldn't have made it."

Father Miller did services in Skagway, so needed to come over anyway. But I'm surprised that night he didn't say to Layton, "I'll just stay in Haines and pray," but not him. He was a humble man of faith, an amazing and beautiful person, through and through. He prayed the rosary all the way over on the flight—there aren't many people like Father Miller. I'm grateful to have known him. God is good—and his goodness shows up in people!

Once we let go of the plane, Layton started right off, and the wind literally picked his plane up in the air like a kite. Amazing, but he made it back to Haines safe and sound. Few pilots could master, or would even try, hazardous flights like Layton. There are reasons people said, "Layton would fly when the crows were walking."

It was some hours later when Frank drove up on the railroad tracks up the mountain with the D-6 cat. Boy, he could handle equipment! He did get the train and the crew out of the snow slide, and were they ever happy and grateful to see him! Those guys were black as aces from shoveling coal and keeping that boiler going. They had been there three days, and all you could see was their white teeth and their eyes. They were covered black from coal dust. Of all the things they could have wanted when they got down from the mountain, they wanted a toothbrush.

Some had wives and girlfriends to see, but first they wanted to brush their teeth. Kind of surprising, from a group of hard core guys, that it wasn't a shot of whiskey. We had quite a party at the Pack Train that night (a last stop for gold miners before they head up dead Horse Canyon.) Every person there was ecstatic!

Happy, happy, campers, all around, that winter night in Skagway!

PRAYER and LIFE'S PATH

"My steps have held to your paths; my feet have not stumbled."—Psalm 17:5

I've struggled, I've scrapped, but I've stayed on the path you have for me Lord.

I pray that each of us look around today—and ask ourselves, "Who is the person who helped me stay on the path God has for me? Who can I help do the same?

Jesus, show us the way, one of positive direction, to know the freedom of your peace and joy! Amen.

Hair, Hide, Guts and Feathers
Mad Raft Race—Haines 4th of July—
Alaska Style

1961-2011—A Fifty Year Tradition

One of my favorite books (and movies) of all time, besides the Bible, is *Lonesome Dove*. The events and characters are in a class by themselves—some replicate my fifty plus years living in Alaska, and the realities of life on my family farm and ranch in Montana. It seems to me that the personalities I've known and the life happenings I've experienced could create a best-selling Western series, despite a century of difference in time.

Quote from, *Lonesome Dove:*

Woodrow Call: *"We come to this place to make money. They wasn't nothin' about fun in the deal."*

Gus McCrae: *"What are you talkin' about? You don't even like money. You like money even less than you like fun, if that's possible."*

The Mad Raft Race has been a fantastic, fun, and somewhat risky tradition in Haines for years! I came up with the idea, and have been one of the organizers for decades. Our 4th of July is not complete without it. It's one of the favorite traditions in Haines, but we had a very close call in July, 2011—a teenage girl, a tourist, almost drowned, so we're tightening up some of the rules. We didn't have any list of rules for a long time, as you can imagine. Praise God this young girl survived; it has to be safe. But that year God allowed it to go right down to the wire—pretty scary and stressful for everyone.

I pray before the race, but even so, the fifty year tradition may have run its course. Hope not, but we'll see!

In the "North to Alaska" chapter, after completing my stint in the Navy, I've told about how I ended up moving to Alaska in 1961. In my twenties, I drove up with several guys and my good friend, Frank Young, who grew up in Haines.

Driving around, shortly after I first got here, we drove out to Lutak, a busy ferry terminal, and Chilkook Lake. It's a picturesque scene right out of the movies—magnificent crystal blue lake, surrounded by mountains, with white tips of snow that remain year-round. They seem to be pointing to heaven. Quartz boulders, the waterfalls and trees are incredible to look at as a person floats along.

The first summer living in Haines, the 4th of July celebrations were coming up—Frank told us how the towns people celebrated and played ball, had games and races, and many of the traditional USA celebrations . . . and a Strawberry Festival with Mary Meacock's strawberries that were as big as tea cups—you do have to see and taste them to believe it!

Standing out at Chilkoot Lake, looking at the outlet that flows from there to the bay, I had an idea and said to Frank, "That would be a perfect place to have a raft race. We could start at the lake, paddle toward the outlet, and from there race two to three miles to the Chilkoot River Bridge. We could have a race for anyone who wants to join in, and *in anything that floats.*

The race proved to be a challenge right from the get-go. When you leave the lake, for about one hundred yards, a rafter has to stay on the left side, because there's lots of rock and tree logs in the river, on the right side. Also, the rapids are good ones—it is no beginners course.

The first year, to get people interested, we needed prize money, so we began talking up our idea of a raft race around town, with the loggers, fisherman's, orangutans (you know the type who will do most anything)—everyone who would listen! We decided to call it, "The Mad Raft Race," with a prize for the winner of one hundred dollars; a pretty good cash prize in 1961.

We didn't have any restrictions—every man or woman for himself. Leo Smith and Steve Gary got a tire out of his skidder—a great big tire, had some poles to maneuver with, and they went down in that. There were all kinds of kayaks and canoes. Man made rafts. I even had a raft made of Styrofoam once. I had been on the rowing team in the Navy, but it wasn't quite like floating on a rapid, cold Alaskan river.

People, nearly the whole town, lined up along the river to watch, even the first year. The river doesn't look too dangerous, but it is really deep when the tide comes in. The rocks and boulders in it are all sizes, some as big as cars. Sometimes they are seen from above, sometimes not.

My first time to raft the river, I went down it with another guy; we had the bright idea of trying to do it in a canoe. He wasn't much better than me and we wrapped that canoe around a rock in no time. The thing tipped over and we were side-ways in the river. Water filled the canoe, and it stayed stuck around the rock. We could not get that thing off to finish the race, so we just swam back to the side and walked down to the bridge.

Those races in the first years were exciting—and still are! In fifty years, there's only been a few we haven't had it. A couple of guys in a kayak won the first race! Made sense—I guess *they* knew what they were doing!

Visit Darryl Johnson—Videographer/Photographer/Filmmaker. The "Mad Raft Race" and other video promotion pertaining to this book, Erwin Hertz and his story can be seen at: http://www.scenefrommemory.com http://scenefrommemory.com/wp/

A FEW FACTS ABOUT HAINES, ALASKA

Visit: http://haines.ak.us/funfacts

- Haines is home to the historical US Military Base, Fort William H. Seward, over 100 years old.
- Haines is your shortest gateway to Glacier Bay National Park.
- Population is 2400, 1897 dogs, 4000 eagles (in fall), and 260 species of birds.
- Haines goes hand in hand with arctic tundra and temperate rain forest.
- Best kept secret in Haines is the large number of artists producing art recognized around the world.
- Haines borders 20 million acres of protected areas of wilderness, the worlds' largest.
- Haines and Skagway are 14 miles apart by water; 350 miles by road which is the Golden Circle Route.
- The Disney movie, "White Fang" was filmed entirely in Haines in 1991.
- Tlingit's were the first settlers to the area and called Haines "Dei-shu" meaning "The End of the Trail." The area is still rich with Tlingit culture and history.
- The Dalton Trail, also known as the Tlingit "grease trail," came through Haines and was not only one of the first routes to the gold rush but also a toll road.
- Both the Big Nugget Mine and Porcupine Mine, featured in Discovery Channel's "Gold Rush" show, are located in Haines.

Haines Convention and Visitors Bureau (email: hcvb@haines.ak.us)

P.O. Box 530
122 Second Avenue
Haines AK 99827
907-766-2234
800-458-3579

CHAPTER 8

LOGGING ACCIDENT AND A BIG TREE WHOMP!

For you have delivered my soul from death.
Have you not *kept* my feet from falling, that I may
walk before God in the light of the living?
—Psalm 56:13 (NKJ)

It's been said, "If it ain't broke don't fix it!
The problem—it was broke!
—Erwin Hertz

I didn't know what hit me, but I'll never forget how it sounded—a deafening *WHOMP!* My unforeseen logging accident happened in December, 1964. I was twenty-eight years old, newly married, and my wife, Georgia, was eight months pregnant. In Haines, Alaska, it was white and frozen like any other winter morning—and 30-degrees below zero. I was working on a mountain above Mosquito Lake, thirty miles from Haines.

My logging partner, Pat, was falling timber with me, near the logging road. I fell two trees and began to limb them. The cat skinner, Don, was waiting for me to finish so he could haul them off to the mill. While he waited, he worked to remove a rotten tree that leaned away from me—about three feet on the stump, six inches on top, and 120 feet tall.

As he drove the cat forward, the tree had other ideas, and it unexpectedly veered backward over the top of Don's cat. He and the others yelled, trying to get my attention, but with my chainsaw going full force, I didn't hear a thing . . . except the unmistakable *"WHOMP"* sound—the fall and thud of the tree hitting ground. My transition was instantaneous—seemingly dead to this world, yet alive in the presence of God.

As it crashed down, it hammered me flat between the two trees I had been limbing. It was unfortunate that I was in the path of the falling tree, yet it was fortunate that I was in the position to fall right between the trees. The downed tree rested its weight across the two trees I was limbing, rather than flattening me. That providential arrangement saved my life.

> "Believe it is possible to solve your problem. Tremendous things happen to the believer. So believe the answer will come. It will."—Norman Vincent Peale

Physically I didn't feel it—absolutely nothing. At impact, my hard hat went spinning into the air about forty feet, or so I was told. As I lay there, other loggers looked at my limp, lifeless body, with the chainsaw handle still clinched in my fist. The running saw had broken off and been hurled into the brush—those few life-changing seconds were dramatic for everyone. In fact, my partner, Pat, came up to where I was laid out, and in his matter-of-fact way said, "He's dead. I'm going back to work." I felt the same, with no emotion about my body laying down there—it could have been a piece of firewood for all I cared.

In that instant, I knew I was in a wonderful place. It didn't matter what Pat said about my condition—he was being realistic. But at the time, I didn't have a care in the world. It seems unusual from an earthly standpoint, but not from a spiritual one. My body was my vehicle to live in the world, but at that point in time and space, I didn't need my physical body that was leveled below me.

The only remembrance I have of the first half hour or so after the accident was what can only be explained as an out-of-body experience—it seemed as if I was twenty-five feet up looking down at my body and the people below. I could see and hear everybody, but I felt like an unemotional observer of the accident scene. I felt peaceful, and oddly I did not feel turmoil or remorse, even though I was madly in love with my wife and we were expecting our first child. I had left my physical body and felt enveloped in God's love and peace that surpasses all understanding. (Philippians 4:7)

I had no overriding desire to return. I had no fear. I felt calm and unrestrained, as if I could travel anywhere in the universe on a thought. It was real—I felt like I had all my faculties. I did not want to come back to earth. Now I know that God had a purpose for me to return.

They say *when you take your last breath here on earth your next breath is in heaven.* I must have been close. In those few minutes, I wasn't thinking about my wife as I normally would have been. Instead I felt confident, with a complete sense of well-being. I had no confusion, but for sure, I also didn't have any control or choice about what came next.

> I've been in God's glory, and there ain't nothing like it!

In a heartbeat (no pun intended) I went back down to the body I saw on the ground—the best way I can explain it is that my spirit reconnected with my physical body in a very orderly way. As this happened, I remember how my feet started kicking in the air. Also, the pain in my body started the very second the kicking occurred. It was as if I was pulling a blanket over my body, and finally laid back, bringing body and soul together—and immediately the excruciatingly painful condition of my physical self throbbed and sunk in.

The tree had come from behind. The blow was not direct, and I had no sensation of the wind being knocked out of me. Had it been a direct hit, obviously I would have been *squashed!* My temperature dropped and I had internal bleeding. Later the doctor told me I would have bled to death if it hadn't been 30-degrees below. *I was fortunate and God was faithful!*

I didn't have a clue about all that was wrong with me, and nobody knew what to do since we were thirty miles from town. The crew was in shock standing over my body. They described to me, later, how it began to turn a shade of purple. They had to do something, so they decided to take me down the mountain, to the sawmill, in the bucket of the steel-tracked cat. The choker setter climbed in the bucket underneath me and held my head as straight as possible, in his lap, as we made our way down that logging road. I remember it clearly.

Once they got me to the sawmill, they made a bed in the back of Big John's station wagon to transport me to Haines, which only has about 1400 year-round residents in the winter. Big John maintains that I died twice more and started breathing again on the longest drive to Haines he'd ever taken. I'm sure he took a breath of relief, like never before, once the doctor at the clinic took over.

How do you walk with a broken back?

The family practitioner got right to it at the clinic in Haines. He patched me up the best he could—but unfortunately the old x-ray machine *did not* show that my back was broken. After all, I was still breathing, and had stood up for them to take the x-ray. How bad could it be?

It's anybody's guess how many rolls of tape the nurses used, but the sprains and bruises were taped up, along with my legs, ribs, and upper body. I turned into a patched up mummy that was quite a site! I slept in my own bed that night, so I figured I'd get well. I slowly began to wobble around on crutches. No big deal!

Most importantly to me was that I could be with Georgia. She was due to deliver soon. Because of a RH Factor scare, she needed to do that down in Juneau. Even though I wasn't in the best shape of my life, it worked out for me to travel down with her.

I laugh now thinking how I had to ask her when she was in labor (lasted twenty-eight hours), "Can you move over and let me lay down?" The nurses probably cringed seeing me stretched out in her sterile bed before the birth!

But best of all, I was there—with Georgia during our son's birth. All in all it went well—we soon flew back home to Haines, on a small airplane with our healthy firstborn son. What a blessing! I felt he and Georgia were more important than any pain or problems I was having from the accident—after all, I still had no idea how seriously I was hurt.

Not too long after, I began to crank up the chainsaw again, working in the woods, at least some. As time went on, I continued to have trouble walking and lots of pain. I knew something else was wrong. We decided it was time to go to a hospital in Seattle—where they had a *real* x-ray machine.

In Seattle, the doctor asked "How did you get in here?"

"I walked in here!" I stated, matter-of-fact.

He stared at me intently. "How did you do that with a broken back?"

"Hmmm . . . yeah," I told him. "I knew there was *something* wrong!" Oddly enough, I felt some relief to finally know why I was having trouble walking and in such terrible pain.

While in the hospital in Seattle, they kept me flat for awhile until they decided what to do. Finally, the lead doctor, an orthopedic surgeon, scheduled back surgery. He split me totally open like a turkey, to try to straighten my spine. (My guts were literally inside out, *but I had no feathers!*)

They removed a wedge shaped chunk of bone from my hip, inserted (drove it in with two pound hammer) into my vertebrae (between the third and fourth lumbar vertebrae) to separate where it had crushed together. They did everything humanly possible to try to restore, realign and heal my broken and crushed vertebrae. My doctor in Seattle was a good guy, but not a miracle worker. I knew I needed to be there for long enough for the bone to set and begin to heal, which had to happen before they could put on the cast.

The first night after surgery, in Seattle, I was agitated and restless—the meds, pain, and pain killers had me all stirred up. When I fully woke up, I saw that I was hooked up to everything imaginable. Most of us have been there at one time or another. I climbed out of bed, and in my unstable condition along with the influence from pain killer meds, I began 'talking and walking' down the hall.

In my head, for whatever reason I had to find the nurse's station, so I dragged IV's, blood infusion and all the "stuff," down the quiet, night-time hall until I found the nurses. They were upset with me, so in return I got strapped in my bed. They were seriously concerned I had just ruined all the work the doctors had done! It felt to me like they had *ruined all my fun and games!* Seriously, I was in a post-op fog from anesthesia and meds—I was kind of out of it, and couldn't have helped them if I tried. It was probably none too soon for them when they released me from the University of Washington hospital.

I was pretty much laid up for one and one-half years, trying everything that might help. After all, I had the back fusion from the front—I'd been taken apart and put back together! When all was said and done I had a hard time getting my life back together. Georgia, Stony, and I went to Montana to live on the family farm for a long period of time.

I had to be put on the plane in Seattle with a forklift; after the surgery/fusion, my original cast weighed seventy-five pounds, and it went from my ankle to my chin. I wore it for six months—*miserable!* I continued to have lots of pain, and could only inch along like a plump, heavy caterpillar when I walked. But still, I wanted to do all I could—I didn't feel like I was *sick* just because I had a broken back.

Eventually I told my wife, Georgia, "I'm tired of taking pills. These pills make me feel sick all the time. I'm not going to take them anymore—anti-inflammatory, pain, and antibiotic drugs . . . because I broke my back."

I frustrated my doctor, but he still became a friend. I began to hang upside down on a bar in the basement of our house with that heavy cast on. I feel pretty sure it helped much more to realign my spine than the six operations that the doctors recommended I schedule.

No more surgery!

I had a family to support, yet I needed physical support with the cast on, so for awhile we lived back at the family ranch in Montana; Georgia, Stony (Erwin Hertz, Jr.), and our daughter Lisa, who was born a year later. Nobody was living in the old house there. It needed lots of work, and fixing up, but Georgia got excited, worked hard to furnish and refinish floors and walls. We made it work. The house sat up on top of the hill, looking out over the whole valley—beautiful time of life in lots of ways—pleasant, loving memories.

I got a big straw hat to wear in the summer; on my crutches and a cane, I walked around looking like a grand plantation owner (unless you looked at the cast below my hat). We fished, had picnics. It was a laid back family time.

I couldn't consistently work hard, at physical jobs. Even though I could have never worked again, received disability or something, but I *wanted* to work. While we were staying in the ranch in Montana, I went back and forth on the train from Missoula to Seattle for cast changes and treatments, what seemed like forever at times.

A forklift still had to be used to get me on and off my airplane. The airlines wanted me to come up with one of my own. *I didn't have one handy*, so I figured there were enough farmers in this area I'd grown up in, I could ask them for help. It was nothing for them to help get me off the plane—after all, even with the cast on I was lighter than a cow, and less ornery than a bull!

As I healed, slowly, I was weaned off the casts—with each new one made a little bit smaller. I'm a German boy who always worked hard and never quit trying, but even so, I had a really tough time.

I'm not a rebel, and don't dislike doctors, but I trusted my instincts as time wore on with my back trouble. I don't know why the fusion didn't hold, but within ten years, the whole thing disintegrated and collapsed. The doctors wanted to fuse my back again and I said, "No!" I went round and round with them, even though I knew they were trying to do the best they could.

They would look at me and say, "Well, you have a broken back." Again I'd say, "Yeah!" Always lots more tests, and always the same report. "You are stronger than people with good backs!" I said, "Yeah, I know!"

> I admit it took guts for me to get through it. I'm sure glad God gave me some.

Besides all the doctors and the surgeries they suggested (that I wouldn't agree to), I continued with different things—hanging upside down, reversing gravity, to ease the pain. I started exercising, walking and running to keep my strength up. I even entered a few logging contests during this time. Doctors always asked, "Do you need pain pills?" I didn't want to take them. I appreciated the doctors' efforts, but I listened to my body, and my "pain treatment" was to jump in the frigid waters of Lynn Canal, even in the winter time. Now that took the pain away, and *made my hair stand up!* That was the beginning of the "Polar Bear Club" In Haines.

Finally I found a doctor in San Francisco, a young doctor, and a very good orthopedic surgeon and back specialist. You can imagine how much I liked him when he said, "You don't have to fuse it again! I said, "Wow . . . thank you! That's what I want! I do not want another fusion or operation! I tried that and it didn't work!"

I will always remember his words. "I can make you a back brace that you can wear more easily. You will have to wear it every day for a year, and then we will reassess how you're doing." He made me a back brace that was fantastic.

He said, "You don't have to wear it at night, but I recommend patients wear it for 24-hours-a-day for a solid year." I asked him if I could possibly take it off at night, and he said, "Fine, but you have to put it on first thing in the morning."

Superman!

I could hardly take a drink of water the brace was so tight, but it still felt like a million dollars. Man, I walked around with my chest sticking out. One day, a buddy walked up and poked me in the gut really hard, but with the brace on, his fist hit the hard plastic front. He yelled, "I broke my fist." I laughed and said, "Well I told you I had good muscles."

He questioned me. "What in the hell do you have on?" I pulled my shirt up and showed him the brace. He said, "My God!" (It looked like my muscles rippled under my shirt, but sorry to say, it was just the brace, but it sure pushed everything back in the right place. (Chuckle)

I'd walk around town with my chest sticking out like a rooster, and old loggers would come up and say, "What the hell is the matter with you! You're walking around like you are Superman!" I'd laugh and say, "Well I am!"

I did feel like Superman! The latest doctor and the brace changed my life. I became even more disciplined about regular exercise. Man, I started skiing, mountain climbing and goat hunting. I could lift and do normal stuff again. I loved down-hill skiing and I took some really bad spills, but I knew I was safe with that brace on. That wasn't terribly smart of me to assume that the brace would save me. I did wear the brace just as the doctor prescribed—for the whole year, and I loved it—even though I looked like a puffed up pigeon.

That brace became like an old friend that gave me security *and the ability to live life!* I did not want it off. When they took it off, I felt like a turtle who had just lost his shell, and part of himself. (Chuckle) I felt fragile and vulnerable without it!

I did take it off every day and walk around to do some things, and then I would put it back on. I actually wore it for fifteen months. I just kept taking it off, little by little . . . by little, each time I regained more of my physical abilities. Really great!

During the challenges of that time in my life, there were many good things that came to me—valuable, peaceful and memorable family times spent with my wife, Georgia, and our new baby boy, Stony. (His name is Erwin Hertz Jr., but how he got his nickname is another story.) Then Lisa was born, and our family grew. My days were a mix of physical challenges, but the days were filled with many blessings I'll always remember.

I did lots of fishing, and that's never a bad thing. Ice fishing in the winter in the reservoir in Montana, and in Alaska. The brace was light compared to the original cast that was so heavy I could hardly get down to the water—seems to me that *turtles don't have nearly such a hard time.*

Big memories from little events

I knew if I was living and breathing God had a purpose for me. *Amen!* My physical limitations allowed me to enjoy the everyday things many men don't get the opportunity to take—time with Georgia and Stony, then Lisa. My family brought me great comfort during those early years when I was unable to work and achieve all I wanted.

I still smile remembering a time when Stony was small, and all the ordinary stuff we got to do together. Once I had his little toddler legs standing on my legs while driving the truck. He was holding onto the steering wheel. I didn't realize his legs were stuck down in my cast and we almost ran off the road into the reservoir. Not good! *Just two kids having fun!*

We also got our first dog. I've always felt kids and dogs go together like cheese and crackers. I got Stony a German Shepherd pup, we named "Rattler." Well, Stony was just a pup, too, and didn't grow as fast, so I had to tie the dog until Stony got bigger and more stable on his feet. In the meantime he'd get all tangled up in the rope, but before long they could run and romp together. *Yep, cheese and crackers!*

Once we were living back in Haines, life went on. I could share many humorous stories, but I'll end this chapter with just one. Growing up on the farm, I learned how to castrate beef and pigs, and I began to castrate dogs and cats for people in Haines. My friend, Frank, who was now a chiropractor, frequently helped me out with my back. I felt like an amateur chiropractor, getting firsthand "training" by the day, due to the problems with my back. My friend, Frank, now the "doc," even let me practice techniques on him, which in-turn I would practice on others! One day I drove into my driveway and someone had hung a sign from a golden chain on my door—"Castrating Chiropractor." Things like this happen *only in Alaska, or maybe just to me, I don't know!*

Since I didn't take my new title hung on the door too seriously, I decided to begin a new career, one that I could handle with the challenges with my back. I decided to put my electrical training and the education I had received in the Navy to good use—I got serious about beginning an electrical business, and it has served me well. My business is still thriving today, though I'm slowing down. I guess at seventy-six that really is okay.

PRAYER and FAITH

So He said, "Come." And when Peter had come down out of the boat, he walked on the water to go to Jesus. Matthew 14:29

One day, in Haines, the people in my prayer chain were feeling all bogged down. I prayed that each one of us would remember what the word of God tells us. Like Peter, we are asked to have faith—to get out of the boat, keep our eyes on Jesus and trust we can walk on water. Every new sunrise, we can make the choice to begin our day by looking to Jesus, keep our eyes on him—whatever I face, *or you face.* With Jesus alongside it is possible to walk on water, *and not sink.* Praise you, Lord! Amen.

Thank you, Jesus . . . that you are always there to hold us up. Amen.

Hair, Hide, Guts and Feathers
1963
Logging Camp—Any Time for Moose Hunting? Sure

It was moose hunting season, but logging camp is all about work, and there was no time for hunting. I was driving log truck. It was an old-timer, had seen a lot of miles and better days, but still started up and got the job done.

As I was coming in with a load one day, a moose crossed the road. I hadn't gone moose hunting out there, but after seeing it I put my rifle in the truck and kept a watch out for them as I drove loads. Fairly new to Alaska, I really wanted to see another one of those amazing creatures again. I got so excited thinking that I might have a chance to get one. I figured if I ever saw one pretty close to the road, I would stop, and go after it to get a shot.

Another day I was driving back to camp after dumping a load, and a bull and two cows crossed the road. *What should I do?* I figured this was as good of a place and time as any to shoot one. I had to get the truck back, so I thought it would be simple enough to just shoot the moose, and then take the truck back to get it filled with logs again; since the guys were waiting at the landing.

I shut the truck off, grabbed my rifle and took off after them where they had crossed the road, and gone into the brush. The brush was so thick, and I was running as fast as I could. I knew I had to get to the river flats before they crossed the river. They were in the thick brush, I couldn't see them, and I was running full force.

Sounds weird, but all of a sudden, I ran right into the bull, right into his butt, where he stood in the brush. Seriously, you don't mess with a bull with his cows! Man, he was mad. I came to a screeching halt—he was ready to charge me, and just then I realized one of the cows was behind me. I'd passed right by her since the brush was so thick. I had nowhere to go and no time to do anything!

Not sure how he did it so quick, but that bull moose turned around, he was going to get me—I was so close to him it happened in a few split seconds. Lucky for me, I had my gun in my hands, and when he turned, he came right up against my rifle barrel; it pointed right behind his front leg and his heart. I pulled the trigger and he went down. I had to cut his throat, to be sure he wouldn't get back up again, and also to let him bleed out. He couldn't go far. I had my bull moose *and* no injuries from this close encounter—a little too much adrenalin rush, even for me.

Right away, I took off to the truck since the whole crew would be waiting for it. They'd have a pile of logs ready to load, and the logs had to keep moving or the whole system got clogged. I got out of the truck at camp and had blood on me, and they said, "What happened?"

"I got a moose! I got a moose! And it happened fast."

They shut everything down and all of us headed out to see the moose. The quickest way for me to get the moose back to camp was with a D-6 cat. So, that was what I did. Schaffer (the boss) wasn't there, and the crew all wanted to help me with the moose. I gutted it out—but I won't go into more detail . . . though, as you can imagine, there is more to the story if I were writing this for hunters only.

It was late in the afternoon, and nobody went back to work. This really livened up our work day! The guys all ended up helping me hang it up to let it bleed out. Goes without saying, that is not what we were supposed to be doing in the logging camp, but heck, we were all pretty excited about that bull moose.

The next day, I called (LAB), Layton Bennett. I told him, "Layton, I need you to bring a plane that is big enough to take a huge moose back to Haines." We had a small landing strip on the beach, so Layton flew out in a Super Cub.

A Super Cub will pack a lot of stuff, but I thought he would bring a bigger plane. *Guess not!* I said to him, "Layton, I thought you would bring something bigger. I need to go to town too, to get the meat packed and find a freezer to put it in."

He said, "Well, if you can get it *and you* in here, I can fly it."

I said, "Ok." We had some work cut out for us since it was a big moose; I boned a lot of it out. Another guy, who guided hunting trips, was really good at cutting meat up fast—I couldn't believe it, but he was practically smacking his lips the whole time he was boning it out.

Now the problem—the moose was in, but there wasn't any room for me. Layton said, "Just get in; crawl on top of the meat!"

The top of the airplane was made of sort of a fabric; I squeezed in, and stretched out on top of the meat, bulging up the top of the plane. I had my hands on Layton's shoulders. It was so tight in there, but we flew back to town, making it in *not so graceful* landing fashion! Layton couldn't get the plane quite level, as he landed, since the moose was so big and heavy, but like always, Layton made it work. He could fly anything, anywhere! He deserves all the respect he got during his many years of flying.

I took part of the meat to some friends of mine, and to one of the guys who had a family, and gave it to different folks around town. I didn't have a place in town yet. I was there off-and-on, so just gave it to different people I knew. Really delicious meat, if you are a meat-eater.

Layton flew me back to camp the next day, to go to work. About a day later, the boss, Schaffer, came back to camp. He said, "I heard you took the crew moose hunting."

I sort of smiled, "Yeah, I guess I did!" This was the start of becoming good friends with Schaffer—turned out he was a good boss and a great guy. It was the first time I'd taken a whole crew moose hunting. Heck, when a moose is there you just have to take the shot!

I want to acknowledge L.A.B. Flying Service. This was the oldest Air Taxi service in Alaska, and it was founded in 1956 by Alaska bush pilot pioneer, Layton A. Bennett—L.A.B. Flying Service was an American airline based in Haines, Alaska, U.S. It operated scheduled, charter and sightseeing flights in Southeast Alaska. Its main base was Haines Airport, with a hub at Juneau International Airport—for over fifty years.

CHAPTER 9

GOD IS AND GOD DOES

So he answered and said to me: 'This is the word
of the Lord to Zerubbabel: Not by might nor by
power, but by My Spirit,' says the Lord of hosts.
—Zechariah 4:6

I have been keeping a prayer journal for several years, now
worn and falling apart. In the back of my mind, I wanted
to write a book someday, even though there was a time in
my life I hadn't even read God's book! But that's how
God works. Beyond amazing!
—Erwin Hertz

God's miraculous events continue to happen in my life, and for
those I pray for and with. I've become more serious about a lot of
things, especially the reasons for telling people about who God is
and what he does! It is so wonderful, beyond amazing, what God
has done throughout my life—out and out miracles that I cannot
explain.

God is worthy of PRAISE

The LORD is my strength and song, and
He has become my salvation; He is my God,
and I will praise Him . . .—Exodus 15:2

Divine relationship: I ask people if they read the Bible; many say, "No!" I'm kind, try not to be too much of a pest, but am persistent. I tell them, "The Bible has guidance and answers that fit for exactly where you are in your life, right now, and it fits every situation that you will encounter in this life while you are walking on this earth."

It blows me away that people will not read the Bible, since I don't know what I would do without it. Why not read it and at least give it a try? It's worth the effort, and full of spiritual promises, surprises and treasures. God invites each of us to experience life, and every circumstance of life, in relationship with him right by our side. The Bible helps to tell us who God is; a wise, ever-present helper, and an all-knowing friend. It's sure not easy or fun doing my life without him. I've tried that, maybe you have, too. I teasingly say, "You don't have to go to heaven if you don't want to, but hell doesn't sound too good."

I didn't read the Bible in the Catholic Church growing up. In the Navy, I started to read it for the first time, but I didn't do it seriously. I'm thankful that I was *at least* curious about the book that has more printed copies than any other, and that I did want to know more about God. I know now that was God holding onto me, not letting me go—*and holding out a carrot to me*—which was the Bible and his truth. Within it was exactly what I needed to get to know him more, and to build a real and lasting relationship with God. Today, I am amazed how the Bible, through the Holy Spirit, speaks truth into every aspect of life, every challenge, every joy.

In 1967, a few years after my logging accident, I got very serious about reading the Bible, talking to God, and praying to him—one-on-one. Once I committed myself to God and to reading the Bible, I was surprised how the words on the pages started to make sense. God was faithful to help me learn, and to this day I just keep on, keepin' on, learning more every day. It's so exciting, because there is always more about God to learn and experience. He has plenty of work for us to do on ourselves and for others!

When I first opened the Bible, I felt like I was a kid in first grade all over again. I needed the help of the Holy Spirit. I needed a teacher, of sorts, to be able to read and understand the meaning of the words on the pages. God must have known I had a sincere heart and that I wanted and needed to learn, remember, and apply to my life what I was reading. Yeah, before I knew it I began to appreciate and understand it to the point of being able to help other people do the same. Praise God!

It is life-changing, and always humbling, but to get God's instruction right (yes, there is still right and wrong, black and white) and to personally take on more of his character traits is a lifelong process. I try to help myself by always praying, and taking time each morning to listen. God has inspired me to start writing scripture and prayer in log books, but even without doing it, his many miracles are clear as a bell to me.

At the time I first began reading, one of the concepts that struck me like a sledgehammer was God's desire for us to ask through prayer for what we need. People don't ask! I believe, through my own experiences, people don't have because they don't ask! "Ask, and it will be given to you; seek, and you will find; knock, and it will be opened to you."—Matthew 7:7

I will never get over how prayers are answered when we begin to ask! The Bible says that God cannot and does not mislead us! "He is the Rock, His work is perfect; for all his ways are justice, A God of truth and without injustice; Righteous and upright is he."—Deuteronomy 32:4

People have and always will, try to prove the Bible untrue or wrong. The reality is that those who try to undermine the truth of the Bible have themselves been proven wrong.

God is who he says he is, and the Bible is what he says it is! I'm living proof that people who are serious about studying and applying the word of God, see life-changing results. Absolutely true! If God can do this for me, he can do it for you—just ask!

Thank you Lord; praise God, praise Jesus, and praise the Holy Spirit!

God does give PROTECTION

I will both lie down in peace, and sleep; for you alone, O LORD, make me dwell in safety. —Psalm 4:8

Divine safeguard: In high school, I was out on a horse-riding date with Nita. We had ridden back to her house, and it was getting late—and close to dark. Looking up, I could see big thunder clouds rolling in, and the sky getting grayer and darker. It began to rain. I kind of cringed knowing I had about three miles to ride home.

Thunder roared above me, and lightning flashed all around me. I yelled, "I have to get out of here and get home!"

Geronimo wasn't unusually scared or skittish with lightning, but no horse likes it either. But I felt different—I sure did not want to be outdoors on this wet horse in this lightning storm. I jumped on Geronimo, and he headed for home—fast! Obviously he wanted to get home too! With roars above us, and lightning flashing around us, I hung on to him for all I was worth. I knew it might be tough to stay on, because when he galloped I could feel his every muscle gathering up and working beneath me—boy, he knew how to stretch and run!

It got darker and darker, and we were going full blast for home! Here I was, on this huge horse and we were running beside the road in the soft dirt paths. He knew them well, even in the dark. The telephone poles and power poles were on the trails along the side of the road. He knew that, too. I could see them in the daytime, but he was running full blast and it was dark! As God well knows, with the next flash of lightning, I saw a telephone pole right between his upright ears, right there! It was ten feet or less away, and there it was. As fast as lightning—in a flash we could crash!

I didn't have time to say "save us Lord, or have time to do anything!" To this day, I do not know what happened, because he never swerved or anything. God was watching over me and that horse; that is all I can say!

There is no way that Geronimo could have missed that post, but he never hit it. If he would have hit that it, it would have killed him and probably me, too. "Horrific Crash" would have been the headline in the newspaper. It could have been nothing else as fast as he was going! Another miracle in my life, but it's important for me to say that I don't take God's protection for granted, or chalk it up to luck. He has kept me from harm too many times that are otherwise unexplainable.

I can still see that telephone pole between my horse's ears. I was a boy that God knew needed watching over, so he sent guardian angels, arch angels, and whatever it took. I can't explain it; I just tell it like it happened. Thank you, Lord, for continual protection and for answered prayers; thank you Lord for Geronimo and for who that wonderful horse was in my life—Geronimo meant the world to me.

God is POWER

**Finally, my brethren, be strong in the Lord and
in the power of His might. Put on the whole armor
of God, that you may be able to stand against
the wiles of the devil . . .—Ephesians 6:10-18**

Divine authority: Growing in faith is never boring! I was involved in spiritual warfare before I knew it was spiritual warfare. But I have learned. Still, I wouldn't trade this journey for anything because of what the Father, Son and Holy Spirit have taught me and done in my life.

This life journey isn't always easy, but with God, it is fantastic. There are many dangers, toils and snares, but the next day, if we ask, God provides the power to overcome whatever we face.

One of the realities we have to face is that evil does exist. I had a young friend, David, who is now a lifetime friend. He came to work for me some years ago, and at that time he did not believe in Satan. He is a great guy. He had come to the Lord; God was doing work in him, so I warned him he would be under attack from, Satan, the enemy of God.

He felt "the devil" was just an excuse Christians used when they did things that weren't right. "The devil made me do it," and all that. He felt it was nonsense, and would say to me, "Hertz, he is just something you've dreamed up in your mind, a figment of your imagination!"

Finally one day I said in no uncertain terms, "Sit down; we are going to settle this right now!" I got my Bible from the truck and said, "I will show you where Jesus started his ministry, when he was filled with the Holy Spirit, and then how the devil tried to tempt him for forty days and nights, with kingdoms, glory and authority. Even Jesus fasted and prayed to stand firm on the solid rock of the truth and power of God. So who are we to think we get a free pass from being tempted by Satan when Jesus had to claim God's power to overcome temptation from the devil?"

I read Luke 4:1-4: And the devil said to Him, "If You are the Son of God, command this stone to become bread. But Jesus answered him, saying, "It is written, 'Man shall not live by bread alone, but by every word of God.'"

It seemed to me that David had a chip on his shoulder about Satan; he didn't want to accept the reality of his existence. It wasn't long after that when we were doing an electrical job at the liquor store—there were lots of liquor labels that had to do with evil—may seem like nothing, but words and pictures depicting evil open the door for Satan to squeeze in to our life. That led to more discussion, and David began to see and understand.

I told him, "Satan tries everything against everybody. It's hard to imagine Jesus under attack by Satan! Think about us. We don't have clout like Jesus, and he was really under attack—for forty days and forty nights, and other times, too! It's all written there in the Bible."

I was serious about getting through to David. "David, listen, by the truth of God, Satan is real! He doesn't have any power, but he uses every trick, and has everyone thinking he has power. He makes bad stuff look good, short term. In the long term people realize different—sometimes it's too late."

I told him, "Even Christians don't always know that when Jesus died on the cross, any power Satan may have had, was stripped from him. Now, through the blood of Jesus, and claiming authority in Jesus name, we have power and protection and authority over Satan, on this earth and for all eternity."

We can pray, on our knees before the Lord, to defeat anything that Satan throws our way. Satan did not succeed in tempting Jesus, because Jesus had worship only for his father, God. We must be sure we worship only the Father God, too. It's a good question to ask ourselves? What do we "worship" in life?

When Jesus died on the cross over 2000 years ago, he defeated Satan for our sake. In turn, we must hold fast to Jesus, and the truth of the following versus as our stronghold against the enemy.

"The eternal God is your refuge, and underneath are the everlasting arms; He will thrust out the enemy from before you, and will say, 'Destroy them!'" Deuteronomy 33:27

"In righteousness you shall be established; You shall be far from oppression, for you shall not fear; and from terror, for it shall not come near you." Isaiah 54:14

Just start quoting these verses, and talking about Jesus and his precious blood, and Satan leaves—runs away! He has no power or authority! A surprise to the enemy, and amazing power and grace for us! The enemy comes to kill, but Jesus gives us *life*.

God does bring PEACE

> Be anxious for nothing, but in everything
> by prayer and supplication, with thanksgiving, let
> your requests be made known to God; and the peace
> of God, which surpasses all understanding, will guard
> your hearts and minds through Christ Jesus.
> —Philippians 4: 6-7

Divine appointments: God puts other people of God in our path to help us see truth, find hope, feel cared about, and avoid the snares that can trip us up. Love heals. Peace comes alive in your heart and mind when you know you are loved. You have to love yourself before you can love someone else.

We all have our problems and we think that people don't like us, and that we aren't loved. That is a fallacy. God does love us, and I often tell people, "I love you and God loves you too!" That incredible truth washed over me like a balm at ten years old. "God loves you" only three words, but the most important ones a person can receive and understand.

I am a godfather to four girls, now grown women. If each of us try to make a positive difference in even one other person's life, the world will be a better place. I have been blessed with desire and means to help these four godchildren as they were growing up. I feel God intended me to step in to help them when they had few others to rely upon—I care about them. I did then and do now. I have a Christian commitment to them.

They had a hard life with drinking, neglectful parents, and all that goes along with that horrendous type of upbringing. Their mother was killed when she rolled her car, and the grandparents tried to raise them, but they were too old, so they went back to live with their father. Their dad was always in the bar business—and died an abusive drunk. More than once I said to him, "Get busy living, or get busy dying."

My spiritual journey and growth involved some of the miracles I saw God do in these girls young lives. Marsha says, "Hertz helped us and cared when nobody else did."

Their names are Marsha, Debbie, Sherri, and Sandy. When my wife's sister married the girl's dad, she asked me to be Godfather to them. Though the marriage didn't last, my commitment to be an adult they could rely on remained. The girls did their best to survive! I stepped into the breach several times, sometimes successfully, sometimes not. I continue to pray for these girls—now that they are grown women, my prayers for them have not changed. Every person can make good choices—yesterday's gone—what's the next right choice that brings peace in your life *today?*

Norman Vincent Peale is one of my heroes. I'd like to share this story I read years ago: Dr. Peale told how he was getting on an airplane while leaving a big city where he had been speaking, and a guy came up to him as he was getting on the airplane. The guy looked so hopeless. Dr. Peale said that he was sorry, but didn't have time to talk as he had to get on the airplane.

He quickly, but sincerely, told that guy, "God loves you"! He added, "God loves you, and I love you too!" Then he boarded his flight and left. A few years later, he came back to the same city for a speaking engagement, and little did he know, this same man was sitting in the front row, there to listen to him, and maybe see him.

After he had finished preaching, the guy walked up to him and said, "You don't remember who I am, do you?"

Norman Vincent Peale said, "No, should I?"

He said, "Yes, you were getting on the airplane a few years ago and you told me that you loved me and that God loved me too! I was going to commit suicide that night! Tonight I was hoping I could talk to you and thank you—I was desperate and had no hope! In those few seconds that you spoke to me, I felt God begin to fill me with peace and a sense of hope. My whole life began to change!"

I am so thankful that I know God, and have gone through some challenges that can sometimes help other people. I ask God to help me. And man has he ever helped me! I would not trade my life journey with God. His peace prevailed even when I was suicidal as a teen. The devil will try to steal our peace by sabotaging our faith, hope and love. He will get you down any way he can! Don't let him. Stand on the rock of Jesus!

God does have a PLAN

For I know the thoughts that I think toward you,
says the Lord, thoughts of peace and not of evil,
to give you a future and a hope.
—Jeremiah 29:11

Life Plans. A divine plan may look different than we think or what we plan: *Oh feathers!* When I was in junior high, my five buddies and I decided to go duck hunting. It was an early Saturday morning, and we could squeeze some hunting in before doing our daily chores. We duck hunted on a huge pond on our property. (The farm next to us had been sold, but I didn't know it. Even so, I learned later we still owned half of the pond.)

As we snuck up on the pond, we saw Canadian geese all over the pond. We had never seen geese on it before, and we thought we had struck the mother lode. We all jumped up and shot at them. Nothing happened—they didn't fly—nothing!

Men on the other side of the pond were hollering and waving their arms and told us to quit shooting. "Hey boys, those are our decoys you're shooting!" We felt so stupid; we got out of there really quick. Seems like a farm boy should know better—embarrassing!

Walking back to the truck, we were laughing so hard about shooting plastic decoys. My buddies started goofing around and grabbed one another's hats and tossed them in the air, shooting at the hats.

I didn't want them to shoot my hat, and I could run faster than any of them, so I took off running for the truck. When we got back to the truck, my best buddy grabbed my hat and threw it in the air. This happened fast—it went about ten feet, and I jumped for it and it landed at my feet; at the same time, my buddy pulled the trigger and the .12-gauge shotgun shell did not go off! It would have totally blown off my feet! We took the shell out and looked at it, and it was dented like it had gone off! We loaded the shell back in the gun, pulled the trigger, and it went off the second time! I know now that I was protected; if he'd shot my feet, I could have been crippled for life, or worse—I could have been dead.

Sure glad that God had a plan for me and my life—a different plan than my actions created. Those decoys may have looked like geese, but they weren't. A reminder that I only know what I know, and that's definitely not everything. But thankfully God does, and he is always in the middle of the action to help see his plan for my life come into being, one day at a time! Whichever guardian angel has had duty for me all my life must certainly be a good one! Think about it. Is that true for you too?

God does have a PURPOSE

> **And we know that all things work together for good to those who love God, to those who are the called according to His purpose. —Romans 8:28**

Divine promise, divine purpose: It's hard to understand how God can take the unfit ashes of my life, anybody's life, and create something good from them. Through Jesus and the Holy Spirit, God reaches out and teaches something from each event that's happened, the good and the not so good, or poor choices I've made. He speaks directly through the words in the Bible—in his promises and perfect timing, he reveals the purpose. I'm continually dumbfounded how my messed up stuff does have purpose. It turns the light on to God's goodness working within me. That's a reward I can count on!

After moving to Haines, Alaska in 1961, there were many things that kept me walking towards God, but few things gave me the chance to meet all kinds of guys from every walk of life than when I joined Promise Keepers. You may be familiar with this nondenominational men's ministry group. Promise Keepers is self-described as "a Christ-centered organization dedicated to introducing men to Jesus Christ as their Savior and Lord, helping them to grow as Christians."

The foundation of all that men in Promise Keepers believe and try to do is based on God's promises for every man and woman in the Bible. There are hundreds of them. Understanding and acting on God's promises increase our faith, show we are loved, bring inner hope, and show us the way. In God's promises, we find our life's purpose.

"Your kingdom is an everlasting kingdom, and your dominion endures through all generations. The LORD is trustworthy in all he promises and faithful in all he does."—Psalm 145:13

Men who are part of Promise Keepers are a bunch of ordinary guys who are seeking God as they try to be better husbands, fathers, and better men in general. It may sound easy, but it's not.

In my Promise Keeper group, we all had past problems, and some were still trying to get right. We were made up of men made up of Vietnam vets, ex-jailbirds, boozers, losers, druggies . . . and the list went on. The kind of men that you might imagine would like the more adventurous, remote, outdoors lifestyle of Alaska. Overall there were about thirty of us (pretty good for our little town), but most Saturdays, ten or fifteen would show up. We studied the Bible, with never a shortage of things to pray about—yes, of course we would eat breakfast if we remembered to put money in the kitty!

Our leader was an ex-service member that was exposed to Agent Orange, and his unhealthy liver was evidence of his former alcohol and drugs use. He was a loose-cannon, but wanted to grow with the Lord. He grew spiritually to understand, "righteous anger." Civilization needs law and order, but we understood that sometimes there's a thin line between the two.

He'd gone to jail for his drug-use; I learned that at the first meeting. He also said he had a hard time trusting anyone who hadn't been in jail. Jail time or not, I guess he accepted me, and the rest of them thought I was okay. I'm one of just a few living members left from that group.

The flip-side was our group leader had a sincere craving for God, and a strong desire to understand God's teaching and promises in the Bible. He was the kind of leader that other men would listen to—he'd come to recognize God's purposes in his life after turning away from the self-destruction of his earlier life. We shared a lot over the years, we laughed, and boosted each other up, as we reached for God's will and purpose in each of our lives.

There's an old saying, "Six days of sinning, one day of praying, don't give you good odds of going to heaven." Not to be judgmental, but we know there are those who look good as they go to church every Sunday—*praying on that day*—but aren't even believers, or don't live a Christian life the rest of the week.

One thing I learned when I was in Promise Keepers was that all of us, to the last man, had tried everything that you can imagine on this earth. Each man had plenty of previous days not living how God would want—we'd seen the good, the bad, and the indifferent. We had seen it all, and we'd done it all—the bad, ugly, *and now we were trying to do the good.*

> I used to ride rodeo, and back then I was sure that I was going to hell on horseback. Walking wasn't fast enough!

Now we prayed. We tried to live every day to God's glory. We'd been there and done it the other way, and *not too well!* It didn't work. *By ourselves* we had tried everything we knew how to be better men, have better lives and relationships, but we couldn't quite see the purpose of our life in the scheme of things, or how we could change. Nothing seemed to make it clear, until we began meeting, and over the years we saw our prayers reveal God's work inside us, and we felt restored, renewed and more fulfilled in our purpose on this earth.

I am so thankful for that group of men in my life. There are only two of us left and at least once a week we still get together and pray . . . for our nation, people in our community, our families, our circumstances and ourselves. We have our Promise Keeper meetings in the back of a bar in Haines where people can come and talk to us. We are no different than them. We're just ordinary men, except we've got Jesus among us, and long ago accepted all that Jesus did for us. He gave his life, his blood, to give us eternal life, and a joyful, peaceful life while on this earth.

Some people in the bar are curious, some come and pray with us, and some ask for healing. Others come and talk to us upset and crying. We help anybody the best we can with what we have. God has helped all of us in some way, shape or form—*that's life!*

PRAYER and GOD'S ACTIVITY in YOUR LIFE

A Praise Spoken from King David in Psalms!

"Deep calls unto deep at the noise of Your waterfalls; all Your waves and billows have gone over me. The Lord will command His loving-kindness in the daytime, and in the night His song shall be with me—A prayer to the God of my life."—Psalm 42: 7-8

Lord we praise your faithfulness to us. We watch for your hand that guides the way, every day. Amen.

Hair, Hide, Guts and Feathers
1963
God is in Control—One Crazy Ride

It was about 7:00 p.m. and I was working in a logging camp about thirty miles from Haines, at "Horton Point." I called LAB Flying; the owner Layton A. Bennett answered.

"Layton, two of us need to fly into Haines." He asked me if the wind was blowing, and if there were swells on the water. I said, "Big ones; big time!"

"Okay, meet me on the runway on the beach, right away." The wind was blowing at major storm force; the trees limbs bent, blowing back and forth. We had to avoid falling branches and whipping trees, so we needed to get completely out of the trees to walk. We headed to the beach where he was going to land.

When we stepped out of the trees onto the beach, there was Layton practically skimming over the top of us in his 4-passenger airplane. He had to bring that plane down, *now!* We jumped back in the trees since the prop came close to cutting us to pieces. He was trying to land at the same time we hit the beach. He had no choice, and we had no clue he was right there; we couldn't hear anything over the noise from the wind, water and trees.

He set the airplane down on the beach, opened the door and yelled, "Get in here. We've got to get out of here *right now!*" We ran and jumped in the plane.

He yelled again, even louder. "Get those seatbelts on as tight as you can!" The airplane was bucking and scooting around like crazy. He took off immediately with the wind forcing one side of the plane to dip against the trees, and in a split second, it was dipping towards the water in the bay—again and again it went back and forth—in the trees, towards the water, in the trees, towards the water! I thought we were going in the water, for sure. That plane should have rolled up into a roll of scrap iron; I couldn't believe it didn't.

The next thing I knew the plane seemed to be roaring louder than the wind, and we had trees all around. Layton gave it his all, had the plane going full blast. We were like a chip in a hurricane. Layton never stopped flying like the incredible pilot he was—I've never experienced anything like it. How the wings stayed on that airplane I'll never know. I've never had a ride like that! It was scarier, and felt bumpier than when I rolled over a car, and another time when a horse rolled over me when I was rough riding in the rodeo.

Layton is a famous bush pilot, and I know if we had not been flying with him, we would not be here to tell the story. After we landed in Haines, he told us, "That is the closest I've ever come to not making it!" And he was a pilot "who taught pilots" in World War II.

Sometime later, I asked him if he believed in God. He said, "Yes." I told him about my walk with God. So there's no other explanation—it must have been God keeping those wings on. No question it wasn't our time to go, because that was some crazy, crazy ride.

CHAPTER 10

GIFT OF FAMILY— MY CHILDREN

Children are a heritage from the LORD,
offspring a reward from him.
—Psalm 127:3

I could have written this whole book about my great kids.
For crying out loud, I wish I'd had twenty of them, if they
were all like my first four.
—Erwin Hertz

I've lived life, that's for sure, and for the most part it's been a good and full one—I sure wouldn't trade it for any other person's life. I am thankful for every day of it. My children are my greatest earthly gift, and they always will be. They mean far more than any accomplishment, or and amount of dollars in my pocket. I am so very proud of each one of them.

I'm a guy, but I can admit it, I have "empty nest syndrome!" I miss having my kids living at home. *I know, I know*—they had to grow up, there's no stopping it. But I miss all the fun we had together in this house and out—the learning and laughter, games we played; the arguments and tears, ping pong and tennis; and our time doing all kinds of family stuff together; outdoor sports, and team sports; fires and food on the beach, bicycling, hunting and fishing, family trips to Hawaii . . . and of course the crazy logging competitions. I wasn't a perfect dad, or a perfect man, but I started each day trying to be the best dad, best man I could—with God's help.

Directly to my kids I want to say: As I write about my life in this book, it's you three adult "kids" *and* Jesse that stand out—far and away, you are more important than anything else on this earth. Living life with you has always kept me scrambling—trying to keep up. You know me; I'm always up for a challenge. Raising kids has plenty of that, especially with multi-talented, strong-willed kids like the three of you. You would probably say I am a little stubborn and strong-willed, too. I'm glad to say that you never have lacked confidence, at least that I could ever see.

I give credit to your mother for your finesse, and that you got her smarts and brains; no doubt your determined spirit, physical fitness and endurance came from both of us—your German heritage being a strongpoint. Yes, *I know*, it's a blessing, sometimes a curse. But you can feel good that your Grandpa and Grandma Hertz are looking down on you, smiling and very happy about the incredible individuals you are.

As you well know, growing up in Alaska is not like most places—it offers unique opportunities. Wow, you girls can do nearly everything a man can do. You tell me I raised you like boys, so I guess you've got it all! Besides being athletic and physically capable, you're industrious and smart; you are great women. Stony, there's nothing you can't do whenever someone asks you to do it. And technology and electrical work; your abilities in those areas leave me more than impressed. With fishing and hunting (especially bear), there is no other person I'd rather have by my side. You can always be depended on in a jam.

> I love each of my kids very much, and not just for the talented things they are able do, but who they are as people

Every man wants to make a difference and leave something meaningful behind. Guess what? *You kids are it!* I can't say enough good things about you three. You know how proud I am of you. I pray you know how I feel—"thank you" for being exactly who you are—you are all the gifts I need in my lifetime!

Always know how much you mean to me—"I love you." Those are words I didn't hear as a kid, so I can't say them enough to you, no matter how old you are. It's a relief to write it down for posterity, not that I expect you'll forget how much I love you, and how proud I am of you. Here's something else that may surprise you. I'm still learning from you, and once-in-a-while I hope you still feel that you learn a few things from the ol' man. I love you, Stony, Lisa, Mary . . . and for sure, we all love and miss Jesse.

I remember . . . When the boys were in junior high school, we'd go in a boat across the river at Ten Mile, where there are lots of slews. We'd glide along into the slews and little creeks by canoe, sometimes kayak. Stony loved it. He would sit behind, "very quiet" in the kayak, waiting and watching for ducks and birds. He could shoot them over my shoulder. We had so much fun doing that together.

One day, Jesse wanted to go out with us too, even though it took me awhile to understand that he didn't want to hunt; he couldn't shoot birds or animals. On this particular day out in the boat, the geese were flying over, and I shot, knocking one down. The other one was flying around there, and I was going to shoot it.

Jesse turned to me frowning, and said, "Dad, they mate for life!" I said, "Ahhh, Jessie. It's a fine time to tell me that now. The other one is already dead!" I didn't know that geese mated for life. Jessie's loving heart for people and other living things was evident in everything he did. *Beautiful!*

To this day, in my eyes, you are perfect children. (Not in the sense of never making mistakes or doing anything wrong, but the fact that you are great human beings, adding good things, of yourself, to this world.) You are alike; you are different! Yet, I see you as extensions of one another . . . and of your mother and me. Life doesn't get much better than that.

My family—high spirited and full of life

I proposed to my wife, Georgia, on the third date. She was definitely *the one!* I loved being married, and treasure the forty years I was married to her. Together, we had everything, and on top of that we made really *great children*—as I said, I wish now I had many more just like the ones I already have. We both wanted more kids, but as timing would have it, when Georgia wanted more, *I didn't*, and when I came around to wanting more, *she didn't!*

The deepest regret of my life is that we are now divorced. It's not easy, in fact it's one of the greatest sorrows that I live with, and it always will be. Looking back, I know we both made mistakes, every couple does. I put my business and work in front of my marriage *and* in front of God!

I worked too much. Some of my jobs were "panic jobs" and unfortunately those happened on Sundays, too. Electrical problems don't discriminate. I didn't' feel I could say, "I will come on Monday!" I was wrong, sometimes I should have said "no." I wish I'd woken up sooner about my priorities, and gotten them right—God, my family, then business—if so, my life might be different today.

I seemed to take on too much, and in doing that, I lost time spent with Georgia. I probably volunteered too much in the community, pushed being out of the house too far. I made mistakes.

I prayed to turn my marriage around, and said, "Lord, you are the only one that can make this marriage work again!" God is in charge today, and he was then. I think I made life impossible for my wife—*sometimes I think that I loved her so much that I drove her crazy!* We had some wonderful years together and with the kids—so many blessings from God, and I will always be thankful. But as I write this today, we are divorced. Only God knows what tomorrow will bring. I must leave that up to him. I know without the Lord, I'd be just be blowin' in the wind.

My kids

Top row—Jesse, Stony & Bottom row—Mary, Lisa

Top row—Mary, Jesse, Hertz
Bottom row—Stony, Lisa, Georgia

**Other things may change us, but we start and
end with the family.**—Anthony Brandt

I plodded along to accomplish what I did in life. It didn't always come easy. But my kids are better—they are smart, good-looking and talented. They are more responsible and skilled than I would ever have hoped and dreamed they would be. Even my dad, who didn't talk about how he felt, or give compliments, said, "Your kids are really something." What he said may seem small, but my kids know *it is big*, coming from their Grandpa Hertz.

Erwin Hertz, Jr., our first child, a son, nicknamed "Stony"

Our first child and first son, was born January 14, 1965, shortly after my serious logging accident—and my back, broken. (See the full story in chapter, "Logging Accident and a Big Tree.") I teased my mother about naming a baby boy after Stony Burke, a famous rodeo rider, but I'd kind of forgotten. I was really just kidding, but when he was just over a year old, we visited her at the farm in Montana. We took the ferry from Haines and drove the rest of the way down from Alaska. Stony was hyper from the long drive, and when we arrived, his little legs ran towards the house where my mother stood. She held out her arms, "Stony, Stony!" *Where did she get that?* It stuck.

I was twenty-eight years old when I had the logging accident. I survived it. I was alive, and it made Stony's birth a couple months later all that more valuable. And everyone who is a parent knows there's nothing quite like the miracle of a child born! After his birth, we took him home on the short flight to Haines, from Juneau. Our little guy sat contented on Georgia's lap, looking out the window of the airplane. It seemed he was already checking out the great big world that was his home, Alaska.

He was the "apple of our eye." But we soon learned we had to do some things different. When he was barely over one year-old, he would trash the house! Whatever he could reach and get to—the cupboards and drawers mostly. His little hands were busy pulling out 'whatever' and throwing it on the floor. Picture it—looked like we'd just been burglarized, empty drawers, and no place to walk on the floor. Stuff everywhere!

One day, I sat down on the floor with him, and put my hand on a book he had just dumped on the floor. I helped him put it back in the drawer; he immediately threw it back on the floor.

I said, "No, Stony," He stood there in his diaper, looking at me, a determined look on his face; I swatted him on his fanny, on the diaper, and put his hand back on the book, then we put it back in the drawer. He was looking at his mother. They both were about to cry. He didn't cry, because the swat on the diaper didn't hurt, but shocked him and hurt his pride. I'll never forget the look on his face, but he never trashed the drawers and cupboards in the house after that. *Glad it worked!*

Stony was good at everything indoors and out, and his younger brother, Jesse (who eventually grew six inches taller), wanted to do everything with Stony, and do everything he could do. He followed around after him, and always wanted to be with him. Wish I had a dollar for every time I said to Stony, "Take Jesse with you." Lots of times he did. He was a good big brother.

Stony had a way of figuring out most anything. He was, *and is,* hardworking, accurate, dependable, and knowledgeable. He does whatever is needed to be done—like his Grandpa did back on the farm.

Stony and Jesse worked together so well throughout their life. One job they loved was for Stan, on his boat, halibut fishing—they'd slap the bait on the hook, and then make a fast release into the ocean! If you have ever done it, you know the drill.

One day, as Jesse put on the bait, that big halibut hook snapped up and went right through his finger. In a split second, Stony was in motion. He flipped open his knife, and cut that line before Jesse was pulled overboard into the frigid water—a person doesn't live long in Alaskan waters. *A close call, but Stony saved the day!*

To get the hook out, Stan and Stony filed the barbs of the hook, then snapped it in-two. Even with a hole in his finger and bleeding, Jesse said, "I don't want to go in!" He was so excited to be with Stony, he sucked it up—so they bandaged it up, and he kept cleaning fish until the day's job was done. Fortunately, it all turned out okay, no infection, no big problem afterward. Proud of both my boys; they grew into good men! Stony is still an avid hunter and fisherman, in Tok, Alaska where he lives today—and when he comes to Haines in the summer to visit and work special jobs.

Now, as adults, I get one up on Stony once-in-a-while. But those days are few-and-far-between He's ahead of the game—he went well beyond anything that was expected of him. He graduated from Oregon Technical Institute, in computer science, in Klamath Falls, Oregon. If it pertains to an electrical system or something technical to do with computers, Stony is your man. He's amazing. Like my brother, Richard, he wants everything to be right. I think Stony is brilliant! He can put that on his resume . . . *and* take it to the bank!

Lisa, our second child and first daughter

Lisa was born on June 1, 1966, while we were living at the family farm in Montana. (I was still recovering from my back injury.) Every dad should have a girl—I was ecstatic!

Her personality and strong will, persuasive and competitive nature was obvious from the beginning. Then she grew into a whiz; very efficient, with a positive and infectious influence over people.

Even as a little kid she wanted to catch the first fish, the biggest fish. She would still be fishing when the rest of us were sitting in the car waiting to go home. And when we started skiing in Juneau, when Lisa was about seven or so—she should have been on the hill with the rope-tow, but somehow she got to an upper slope all by herself, in the Eagle Crest ski area. We had everyone looking for her, but never dreamed she'd get way up to the top. We were frantic!

At last, she turned up at the bottom of the hill. At first she didn't quite know why it was such a big deal; she had confidence, even then. She only got upset because were upset with her.

We knew right away, Lisa was born to be a manager—always a leader. A quality we all want to have, but raising a kid like that, creates situations that are good, and on the flip-side, sometimes a challenge—like the time she took over the sixth grade classroom. I was called to the school by the principal—every parent's dream—*not!*

In grade school, this teacher didn't have control over the class, but Lisa did. For her, it came natural to step-up when other people didn't, even adults. The teacher was a poor one; plenty of educational degrees, but unable to control and manage the kids.

Two of Lisa's teachers lacked class management skills, and twice Lisa stepped up to take control—but it wasn't well received. I told her, "You've got to stop it; sit down and shut up. They aren't going to fire the teacher, but they might throw you out of school!" However, they did quit hiring teachers on resumes alone, and started going to observe and interview in person. I should have known then, that Lisa would get her degree in education—sports/recreation. She went on to become a physical education teacher.

Leadership was an intrinsic part of Lisa's nature whatever she was doing—strong-willed, athletic and hard-charger, good student, smart, and intuitive. That's Lisa.

I remember when the swimming pool opened in Haines. It was a big deal, and Stony and Lisa both were hired as life guards at the pool—our kids all swam like fish. The kids who swam there really liked Lisa when she was in charge of the pool. They also liked to tease her. She hadn't been working there very long when she said, "Dad, what will I do with these kids that get so rowdy at the pool!" She didn't want them to fall down and break their heads open when they were running around the pool.

I said, "Lisa, what do I make you guys do when you got rowdy!"

She said, "You make us do push-ups and run up the hill!"

I replied, "Well, do it!" She tried it, and it worked better than she had even hoped.

The kids loved it when Lisa made them do push-ups. They respected her. I was with her in town one day; we were walking on the sidewalk. A group of boys ran up to her and started doing push-ups right next to her on the side walk. Her personality and enthusiasm was, and is, naturally contagious—a born leader. *Imagine that?*

At that time, Lisa and Stony were the only two life guards that didn't quit or get fired at the new swim pool in Haines. They worked there until they got out of school and left for college. They liked being life guards. As their dad, I know they had a positive impact on the kids at the pool in other ways, too. They are every dad's dream—and every employer's!

When Lisa was student teaching, the boys teased her about going out with them. She settled it easily, without a problem, by telling them, "I'll go out with you if you can do as many pushups as I can." Obviously, that ended that.

Lisa, and her younger sister Mary, are exceptional athletes, determined and hard-headed (in the best sense). It has always been a challenge to find anyone who could do as many push-ups as Lisa. Even when she was in college, she was amazing in so many ways. She met people wherever she went, helping to take care of the gym when she was a college freshman. She worked out and made lots of friends that way; also got college credits for doing it.

Lisa can manage people in most any professional setting. She was hired to run a rehabilitation clinic—she knew just the right therapist for the right patient. When she was in college at Southern Oregon State University, in Ashland, Oregon, she managed apartments while she went to school. We all know what that's like in a college town, especially there. It's a party school—*maybe they all are!* And when working as a landscaping crew leader—the Mexican crews she worked with didn't always understand this white girl who kept them all running, not walking, as they did their work day-in and day-out.

Lisa my beautiful, take charge, daughter also liked hunting and fishing—she could track and "pack in a moose." She would hike in anywhere with us, *or without us,* and still does it today, where she lives in Oregon. She is married, and her husband, Todd, a former football and baseball player, is the perfect husband for her. They are both avid hunters—and even though there aren't any moose to pack in, living in Oregon, there's plenty of deer and elk. Good for you, Lisa! A little tip . . . for those who go hunting with Lisa, don't count on her to do the cooking—*she's there to hunt!*

Lisa and I both remember one time on the river when I should have listened to her. "Dad, I don't think we should go over that."

I replied, "Oh yeah, we can make it!" Instead, I got a wake-up call. We were in a small, overloaded boat on our way to set up camp for moose hunting. The Chilkat and Tarkeen Rivers converged with mighty rapids; soon enough I knew the water was in control, not me!

The boat capsized, we rolled over and over, losing everything in it, including my .338 magnum—my most prized rifle. We couldn't help save each other—we nearly lost our lives as we fought to get gulps of air, then we were rolled and pulled under the water, over and over. I can't say how long we were fighting for our lives, but we escaped hypothermia, so it couldn't have been long.

Stony, always reliable, made his way back to us in his boat. We got the other boat stopped and stabilized—*lessons learned!* One, I should have made a couple trips rather than trying to haul everything over in one trip. Two, I should have listened to Lisa. On that particular day, my judgment was poor—I admit, sometimes I learn lessons the hard way!

Mary, our third child and youngest daughter

Mary was born April 18, 1970, and my youngest son, Jesse, was born, Dec 21, 1971 (You can read more about Jesse in the chapter, "The Loss of My Son, Jessie.")

I discovered raising two daughters was like raising two cougars! I am in awe of the many character strengths they both have. They share many of the same talents, and have always been close—pretty much on the same page!

These talented girls were a two-woman team you didn't want to come up against. For sure, we all knew better than to play a word or board games against Mary and Lisa. They always won! Mary shares lots of similarities with Lisa, but stands out in her own ways, and is her own person, with unique abilities.

As a young woman, Mary came back home to Haines one day and said, "Dad I need to make some money." So, I suggested to her that we go down to Juneau, where the "Gold Rush Days," mining and logging competitions were taking place. They are a big deal, with men and women competing; semi-pros come from all over—with lots of prize money involved. Mary is such a natural athlete I knew we could do well. People knew Mary from her track and basketball accomplishments, but in Juneau, she was not known for these competitions.

I had competed with Stony (and Lisa) in hand-bucking contests and did well, except for the time they brought in dry hemlock logs—supposed to able to saw in less than two minutes, but with hemlock it took me and Stony ten minutes. I said, "This is a logging contest, not an endurance contest!"

Thankfully, Stony and I were always in sync, and we often won—we were a well synchronized sawing team, so right away, I thought that it would be fun for me and Mary to compete together.

It would be very competitive, but I thought we could do really well at it! *Wrong!* We had never done it together, and it was my mistake for suggesting it, without ever practicing with her.

It's called "Ma an' Pa" bucking; and we could not make it work—we buried the teeth of the saw into the wood, but our *yin and yang* did not get in sync. Mary started laughing at the other end. We kept sawing anyway, but our timing was totally off, and we didn't even place. No points, but we were a great clown display—we were laughing at ourselves, thank goodness. Still makes a great story!

Pole climbing is daunting, but I knew Mary could do it—I gave her a crash course, right there. Mary felt pretty spooked about this "high tree climbing." Trees are brought in that are ninety to one hundred feet high. She didn't want to do it, but I kept telling her, "Mary you need to do it!" More points and more money; and for the women, it's safely controlled with a line. (With the men, if we fall, we fall!)

Mary is very coordinated, an athlete, so I kept encouraging her to do it. It ended up that she was very good at it—even though she'd never done it before she got second, competing against seasoned climbers. She could flip that rope up, get her spurs at the right angle—she climbed up in spades! We signed her up for everything that went on over the two days—log-rolling, power-bucking, choker-setting, and more. Mary had never done mining contests, but she flew right through those competitions too.

Mining contests are all done against the clock—and for the steel-rail track contest, Mary ran down the rail with a mining cart—filled it up, ran it back up on the track to dump it—some tough shoveling (rock once, dirt once). She shoveled and pitched it in, and flew right through it since she's strong, and a fast runner. She came in second, and said, "Dad, I didn't do very good." That's Mary, never satisfied unless she wins the *whole* pie, or is number one.

She did win first in everything else she entered! This was in 2001, and I was so proud of how well she did. She was happy, too. She won $1400 over two days. People asked, "Who is that girl?"

Now to go back a few years: Imagine Mary preparing for the Junior Prom. She wasn't a dress person; she didn't like frilly chiffon and lace and things, that girly-girl stuff. Georgia was a dress-maker, so when Mary decided to go, she made a dress for her. Mary tried it on, and didn't like it. They went to town and bought a couple more. Those didn't work either, so they flew down to Juneau, came back with more that they could return if they didn't work. Next was the straw that broke the camel's back—Mary and Georgia wanted to go to Seattle to look for more dresses. Not one dress made or bought so far was the right one—*not one* worked for her!

What did I think? I'm a man, so what do I know? But I'm a dad who loves his daughter, so I told Mary, "Yeah, I think they all look great!"

When they wanted to fly to Seattle to do more dress shopping, I put my foot down. "Mary, you are not going to Seattle! Do you want to go to the prom? If you really want to go, just pick a dress."

"I'm not wealthy, what's next, Mary, Chicago? Just forget the prom if none of these dresses work. Don't go!"

Somebody had to say "no" and it was me. Finally she decided on one of the original dress she'd tried. I guess Mary wanted to wear the pants in the family, but as her dad, I had to wear 'em that time. But looking back, it makes me laugh, and is proof I will never totally understand women.

Mary's a natural athlete and superb in everything she takes on. Years ago, her Uncle Joe knew golf came to her easily, but she could have cared less about it, even though he influenced her to go that direction. He was connected with professional golfing, but it wasn't her passion.

She preferred track and cross country, basketball, or competing in the Alaska State Logging shows; challenging events that are so popular, leftover from the logging heydays. (I always competed, and Stony and Lisa, too.)

In Anchorage, at the state track meets, Mary set new records, most times winning what she entered in the meets. To be pushed harder in high school, Mary sometimes practiced with the boys—in basketball and track—a stickler for improving and increasing her capabilities.

She was able, and we nearly took her excellence in school and sports for granted. These talents were built-in to Mary—from day one she expected so much of herself, way more than we did. Sometimes her intense drive for perfection made it hard for her. She would be disappointed in herself when she didn't reach her own high standards and goals. Yet, in my eyes, she was phenomenal in all that she did.

Both the girls competed in the women's logging competitions: ax-throwing, log rolling, hand-bucking (sawing through the tree trunk with a two-person, bladed saw), and much more, just as we did. It was fun to watch them—they always seemed to take turns winning.

It totally makes sense that she went on to get her degree in Fitness Science at Arizona State University, in Tempe AZ. Mary was a 4.0 *plus* student, and played basketball as a walk-on at Arizona State University, until she chose other pursuits. She was considered to train for the Olympics many times, but for a variety of reasons those opportunities never came together. Willful, intelligent and beautiful, that's Mary. She was named one of the "Top 50" student athletes in America when she was in high school.

You guessed it! Mary is a perfectionist at *everything* she does. She is physically and mentally strong, stubborn, and uncompromising in her competitiveness, focused and multi-talented. She's wonderful! Today, she can train anybody to do anything. I'm very proud, and in awe, of her knowledge and physical abilities. She owns her own business in Bend, Oregon as a trainer for all types of athletes. She works with all ages, from the recreational, amateur, to the professional athlete—for those who have injuries, and those seeking strength training, conditioning, fitness and improved performance.

Mary is passionate about training others, just as she has always been for herself. Her business is doing very well—she works at what she loves, so I never questioned that she would be successful. She and her husband, Alex, seem to be in just the right place, enjoying a great life in Central Oregon.

Jesse: I'm thankful for the time we had with Jesse

Born in 1971—died in an accident in 2000. We miss him, we remember him.

Jesse had a great gift—a genuine love for people

I laugh when I remember asking Jesse once, "What am I, the Master of Ceremonies?" He always had people around him, and he always brought them home. Jesse liked to have fun, just like all kids. He also was the one who could talk the teachers into having a dance or some other activity, so he was the "spokesman" for the kids in school. He was a social planner, bar none.

I chaperoned lots of the activities when the kids were in high school, and helped with most everything that came along. I was on the school board; I helped with baseball, track, basketball, and whatever else the kids were involved in; traveled with the teams to events. I enjoyed it so much. It went by way too fast—*and suddenly, one day, I turned around and they were grown and moving on.*

I pray every day for my family. Join me as you pray for yours.

Like every parent, I want all good people and good things to come their way. I pray that this truth of God takes strong root in their heart: "For God so loved the world that He gave His only begotten Son, that whoever believes in Him should not perish but have everlasting life."—John 3:16

For each of my kids, I want the best the Lord has to offer. It's simple really—I want them to know Jesus loves them, and that he died for them. I want each of them to face each day knowing this, "The Lord is my rock, my fortress, my deliverer, my God, my strength, and whom I will trust.—Psalms 18:2

And I pray that they call on him, *they ask,* knowing he is always there for them. It's true; I see God's hand in people's lives every day. "God is our refuge and strength, a very present help in trouble. Therefore we will not fear, though the earth should change, and though the mountains slip into the heart of the sea . . ."—Psalm 46:1-2 (NASB)

Our truth and hope:

"In My Father's house are many mansions; if it were not so, I would have told you. I go to prepare a place for you. And if I go and prepare a place for you, I will come again and receive you to myself; that where I am, there you may be also."—John 14:2-3

In the journey toward eternal life, we can look forward to the day when we will all be at home together again. I believe, Lord, that I will be saved, and by faith my entire household. There we will see you, and we will see each other and Jesse again. In Jesus name, I pray. Thank you, Lord. Amen.

Hair, Hide, Guts and Feathers
A Loose Cannon and More

My former mother-in-law was a loose cannon—decades ago she even shot up the bar in Haines with her .38-revolver. She caused the guys to run out the door and jump out the open windows. She even managed to shoot two rows of glasses on the shelf in front of the wall mirror. The holes she left in the walls tell the story, and man, it is a long one—the scarred up walls are almost a tourist attraction. For your sake and mine, I'll get right to the point.

If she'd had a double barrel shotgun and hand grenade she could have gotten rid of all three of her son-in-laws, with a bang, all at once—and who knows, that might have ended all her problems!

Squirrel Bait is the Secret

I needed something big and tough that would stay on a big halibut hook. In logging camp, a kid went out and shot a squirrel, and I cut it open and used it to fish for halibut. A squirrel is just the perfect size. With this ideal bait—I got the big one! 250 pounds seven feet long, with steaks a foot and a half thick.

It took awhile to pull it up to the surface—and it took me and six other guys to do it! As a flat, bottom fish, you can't get any leverage. I could go into describing the mechanics of how to catch a halibut, but when all is said and done, it sums it up to say that it feels like quite an accomplishment to catch a big one.

One guy said, "What is it?" I've heard women say, that a halibut "kinda' just floats up." We pulled and pulled from behind the piling until we got it up from the bottom of the bay at the ledge. But once it surfaced, I was in hog heaven! That's the farm boy in me—okay, I guess it's better to call it *halibut* heaven.

Only Idiots Go On Bear Trails after Dark

Not an ordinary, sane person goes out on a bear trail after dark. *I know, I know,* I probably am crazy, but I've done it a few times. One time I went out on the trail to protect a campsite, and put down a wounded bear another guy had left out there. I was able to crawl up behind this bear, as he chewed on his paw, and get the shot.

Another time, I'd nailed a halibut head to a stump, hoping to get a Grizzly. I was all excited about getting that hide. This particular time, I still had no bear, so at midnight I headed back in to camp. Even in Alaska summertime twilight, it gets pretty dark in the deep woods. Running into each other was a big surprise for both of us, when I came upon this bear that was leaving camp (we buried our garbage, but they still came in and dug it up), just as I was coming in on the same trail.

I was on a sprinting run, carrying my .338 Magnum, big time bear rifle, pointed forward and ready to shoot. In a holster under my arm, I carried .44 Magnum for back up. (I never kept the safety on in bear country.) Without warning, a huge Grizzly bear came around a massive boulder on his bear trail, the same one I was on. He was going out, as I was running in. He was loping on all fours, and we ran smack into each other. He came nearly to my neck. *I'm not tall, but he was big!* I swear that bear was just as surprised as I was—the only difference, I had the gun. Instantly, he rose up on two legs, and made a weird yelping sound. I had no time to be afraid; I reacted automatically to survive.

I shot three times at point-blank range directly into his brisket, and then he rolled down the hill. After firing, I loaded up again. I kept shooting at him until he was at the bottom of the hill that ended at the main road. I had to keep shooting to be sure he was dead, since bears can keep coming after a person even when they are shot. Examining him later, I could see how lucky I'd been. The first bullet saved my life, because it went through his heart, shattered his backbone, severed his spinal cord, but came to a stop, still within his hide.

Men from camp came running out with flashlights and lanterns. They said it sounded like three people were shooting, so they knew something was up. Not sure how you'd feel if you'd been in my place, but I knew *one* of us had to go!

Erwin N. Hertz Sr.

Hair, Hide, Guts and Feathers
1963
Logging Camp—No Outhouse
in the Workplace

Quotes from *Lonesome Dove*:

Gus McCrae: "*I could kick you for givin' him all them ideas about Montana. Now we're gonna suffer for the rest of our [damn] lives.*"

Jake Spoon: "*Yeah, I forgot how determined he can get, once an idea takes root.*"

Sound familiar? It does to me. That book, in many parts, feels like I'm reading about my life. Read the chapter, "Born on the Farm" if you haven't yet—combine Montana with German determination and there's enough action for any movie!

One notion, worthy of taking root in young men, are the many benefits gained through stints of hard work in the outdoors, like I experienced in my own life. Every man should spend *at least one month* working in a mountainous logging camp in Montana, Alaska—or *wherever*—to build confidence, responsibility, and skills. There's nothing quite like it (except my time on the farm and in the Navy) to learn how to work hard, get along with people and work as a team, and accomplish the job you're given. Add some conflict, danger, harsh weather, a mix of unique characters and animals—all of these equal personal growth and out-of-the-ordinary experiences and stories to tell grandchildren.

Even in Sarah Palin's Alaska, in 2010, the travelogue television series took the viewers to a remote logging camp in Afognak Island to give a somewhat *solicited* taste of logging camp life. (Side note: I met Sarah Palin, briefly, once in Haines—security everywhere, but I felt God urge me to pray for her, and I told her so. She paused; I said a short prayer, asking God to cover her in the blood of his son, Jesus Christ.)

Believe me, over fifty years ago in the spring of 1963, I found working in Alaskan logging camps an interesting challenge. The camps were crude in more ways than one. Still, I loved the work.

I suppose today there would be a law that would prevent this, but my first logging camp job, didn't have an outhouse. Well, it did, but not any *typical* outhouse. You know what they say, *make it simple, Sam*—so why not just dig a deep hole out in the woods behind the bunkhouse? That'll work! Then put a heavy pole across the hole and a hang a rope down from the tree to hold onto—in case you don't get the picture, the heavy pole across the hole was the toilet seat! That was it.

The guys that "designed" it were tall—I know many of them that were well over six foot four. I was only five foot, eight! Man, it was spooky and wobbly to sit on that pole, on that so-called toilet seat! My feet could not reach out to the edge of the ground around the hole to add balance. You've got the picture, but don't go there, it will make you dizzy!

Working there in the spring of 1963, April Fools' Day was coming up. I'd already seen some of the outrageous jokes the guys played on each other. I had a few thoughts about an outhouse April Fools "joke." I could imagine some guy sitting out on that pole, first thing in the morning, quiet, with birds chirping all around. Wouldn't it be fun to saw that pole about halfway in-two the night before, and leave it for an unsuspecting person? *I know, maybe not!*

I swear I didn't have the guts to do that—I had more smarts than that, even then. The seasoned logging camp guys weren't spooked about much, but I have no doubt I would have ended up head first in that hole if I'd been idiot enough to play that April Fools' joke.

Later on, after I complained enough to the boss, he had me dig a hole and build a regular outhouse around it. I was happy to do it; and a happy camper after that! (Chuckle)

CHAPTER 11

THE LOSS OF MY SON, JESSE "HIS SMILE WILL LIVE FOREVER IN OUR HEARTS."

Call upon Me in the day of trouble; I will
deliver you, and you shall glorify Me.
—Psalm 50:15.

Jesse loved life; and life loved him back.—Erwin Hertz

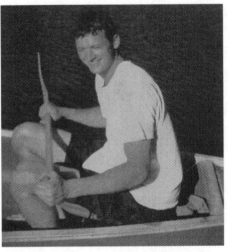

Jesse made the most of every day

My son, Jesse, was born in 1971. It's interesting how he got his name. As a kid, my friends and I were called "The James Gang," since we caught horses out in the Badlands of Montana! And my nickname was Jesse. My wife wanted to name him after me in some way, so we named him Jesse.

As most everyone knows, this life journey isn't always easy—I'm just glad I get to do it with the Lord Jesus. God's promise in the above verse is one I rely on completely—in every circumstance. My youngest son, Jesse died in an accident in the year 2000, at twenty-eight years old, the same age I was when I nearly lost my life (had an out-of-body experience) in the logging accident. The difference, I survived.

Jesse's death was such a shock to me and my family, and the whole town of Haines. Jesse was everybody's favorite; the community loved him—*everybody knew his name,* as they say. We didn't realize how many people's lives he had touched so positively until he was gone—he left a legacy through the people he helped and cared about.

He was very intelligent and good in school; always an energetic, good kid from day one. I remember one of his first days in kindergarten he brought a kid home from school with him, and I asked, "What's going on Jesse?"

He said, "Dad, he didn't have any breakfast!"

I reassured him, "That's okay, we'll feed him!" That was Jesse to a "T." He was tuned in to people and their needs. He noticed them, he cared—and would share his food or anything else he could to show they mattered. I'm so proud of the loving and generous spirit he spread around during his life—always helping people. It had to be Jesus living in Jesse; love and acceptance. And his compassionate heart towards animals—as a family in Alaska, we hunted, but not Jesse. He liked to fish, but he couldn't shoot an animal. He had a tender heart.

It can be hard growing up in a small town where everyone knows you. Jesse was popular and he was a leader. When there was a fight at school, he would get in between the kids that were fighting, and they ended up hitting him instead of each another. I couldn't believe it! I got in fights in school, but not quite like that! Jesse was a rare jewel. Oh man, it was more than hard when he died!

He paid his dues at a very young age. A couple years before he rolled his truck, in 2000, I felt like there was something going to happen in his life—God put it in my heart to pray. An unsettling premonition set in, but I didn't know what it was. I'm so grateful he believed in Jesus. But I prayed he would draw even closer to God, and I talked to him, and pressed the point, "Jesse, something is coming down in your life, and I want you to stay prayed up. I want you to pray every day!"

Jesse said, "Oh Dad, I know all that stuff!"

"I know that you do, Jesse, but I want you to be aware!" And then it happened. Jesse rolled his truck one night after his class reunion party. He was going out to the road to meet his girlfriend, about 2 a.m.

My oldest son, Stony, Hose Captain for the Fire Department, was on the ambulance crew; they arrived at the accident scene with the "jaws of life." The other men would not let Stony go out to the wrecked truck. They said, "It's your brother, and he didn't make it!" Stony came back in to town, and woke me and my wife up with that sad and shocking news.

Jesse was dead! A very gentle spirit; a vivacious person, an athlete—he did extreme sports, skiing, kite boarding, and all kinds of challenging, risky things outdoors. But he loved life and simply wanted to live each day to the fullest.

We don't have a morgue in Haines. Jessie was put in a cold (body) box in the little garage at the back of the fire station. One of the hardest things I ever did in my life was go over there that early morning and see Jesse lying in that cold room.

Hours ago, he was so alive, and now, there he was on that bare, cold slab. I tried to hold him and hug him. It was so terrible. Jesse did risky things, but this reality was the most shocking. He always drove fast; *fast, fast, fast!* We all told him, "Jesse, you drive way too fast!" He was always in a rush, with so many things to do, and places to go, and people to see. How many times had I said to him, "Good grief, Jesse, what is the rush?"

Later that day, I took, Georgia, and our two daughters over to see him. Stony had been there with him already. Oh, my dear God, it was so painful to see them with their brother! The loss and grief . . . it was wrenching, because I love each of my kids with everything I am. Like all parents, I expected to leave this earth before any of them.

It is difficult here in Haines when you have someone close to you die. We got a casket and made the arrangements the same day, because they can't keep the body at the fire station too long. It was amazing that there was a birch casket at Haines Home Building—it was perfect for Jesse. If there is such a thing as a perfect casket for your son—*words can't describe my feelings.*

We put a rosary, photos and other special things in the casket with Jesse. My son-in-law started to put the lid on Jesse's casket. Looking at him in that beautiful birch casket, I said, "Wait, I am going to try to raise Jesse from the dead."

I could not leave Jesse until I prayed over him

With every shred of faith within me, I asked God to raise him from the dead, but I knew, and had to accept, that God had taken him home, ordained his life. At that moment, I realized Jesse was in a far better place. God's peace penetrated my heart, but the grief remained, and the loss of being on this earth without him, will be with me until I meet him again in heaven. It was hard on all of us—my wife, and Jesse's brother and two sisters. Some of you know; you've experienced the loss of a child, too. *May God bless you with peace!*

As hard as it was, when Jesse died, I prayed, "God, Jesse was your child before he was mine. Lord, you trusted Jesse to me, and now I trust him to you. I know that if he is with you; he is where he is supposed to be."

After Jesse's death, I found a log of his writings. He wrote about the people he cared for and loved so much, and those with problems he was trying to help. Jesse made friends with kids that the other kids didn't like to be around. The kind of kids that didn't understand what was wrong with them; Jesse tried to help. He had written about them, evidence of how important his relationships with all kinds of people were in his life.

A headstone: "His smile will live forever in our hearts"

We needed a headstone. Jesse loved the Porcupine Mine (Some of you may have seen it. The Porcupine Mine is featured in Discovery Channel's "Gold Rush" show.) I borrowed a truck, got a bunch of planks and pieces of pipe, and we went up there to get a headstone. We rolled a big piece of granite, just me, Georgia, Stony, Lisa and Mary—all by ourselves. It was something that we could do all together, and be together, *for Jesse.* Oh, man!

I spoke at the funeral, but it was really tough! Then we lowered the casket into the ground. I will never forget having to pry, Mary, our youngest daughter off the casket—she was crying so hard—the whole day was so sad and difficult.

Abraham Lincoln said, "I have been driven many times to my knees with an overwhelming conviction that I had nowhere else to go." That is me. I'm often on my knees before the Lord, but never like the day that I buried my son—only with God's help could I find the strength to do it.

People came—so many, Jesse would have loved it. Finally, when the funeral was over, that evening we had a potluck. I needed to be by myself, get some space. I went down to the shoreline beach, Lynn Canal, down from our house; it is the place I go to walk, and to find peace and solitude.

On my bicycle, I started down to the beach, and I really got going fast down the hill towards the shore and the ferry terminal. *Man, I was smokin'—I was flyin'!*

Jesse came to me, right in my heart—I felt him there with me! I almost ran off the road! Man, I would have been pretty beat up if I'd run off the road going that fast! I was shocked—he was with me, right there, for a few seconds. All I could say was, "Oh my God, Jesse! Jesse! Jesse!" . . . then he was gone.

All I could do was hold on to Jesus and his promises; trust Jesse was with him, and that my family and I could find peace, and the strength within to celebrate all that Jesse was. Memories of him will *never* be taken from us—and they are sweet!

"These things I have spoken to you, that in me you may have peace. In the world you will have tribulation; but be of good cheer, I have overcome the world."—John 16:33

Remembering Jesse

The next year, the kids all came home, and together, we did things that Jesse always liked to do. We went on a picnic at his favorite place down on the beach. We ate hamburgers and went fishing. It was great; ordinary things we did together as a family became extraordinary treasures as together, we remembered Jesse in this way.

Some days, it is hard to go to his gravesite. Sometimes I go there and pray; it is peaceful. And I also pray at the place where Jesse rolled his truck. A bunch of kids built a big monument of stones there; they kept building it higher. Stan Wood and his son really liked Jesse, and had another idea . . .

They wanted to make a memorial for him at the accident site. I said, "No, you can't do that, because the highway department won't like it." So instead, I put a cross in a tree near where his truck rolled; it gives me peace to go there. The intense grief of losing him gets better with time. I purchased a plot next to Jesse, so I can be buried near him when it is my time.

Comfort comes in unexpected ways

Jesse was such a personality; he came back to see me—*he did!* Call it a vision, a dream, I don't know. All I know is that I saw him a few years later, and I cannot begin to explain it! I woke up in the morning—I wasn't awake and I wasn't asleep. He drove up to the back of the house in a pickup that he had bought. (By the way, you can't drive up to the back of my house.)

I did need a pickup; he apparently had one for me. He got out of the cab, walked up and said, "Hi Dad!" I said, "Hi Jesse!" And then he was gone!

It happened just like that. I cannot explain it, but it was real—God's gift to me. *Thank you, Lord.* It was just like Jesse to let me know he was okay. This is another aspect of my journey with God that I won't understand or be able to explain until I get to heaven.

Jessie was going with this beautiful girl at the university in Seattle, and we all really liked her. We hadn't heard from her for a year or two after Jesse died, until she sent me a photo of him. He looked more mature and a little older in the picture, and of all things, it was exactly what Jesse looked like the morning that he drove up to the back of the house, in my vision/dream. Again, I cannot explain it, and I don't make light of it. God works in mysterious ways—*does he ever!*

I knew a lady that would talk to the school kids about Jesus Christ, and about God. She walked up to me one day, after Jesse's accident, and with her two little girls in tow she said, "A lot of the high school kids make fun of me when I try to talk to them about Jesus—and the love of Jesus, but Jesse never did make fun of me!" She added, "Jesse was always so nice to me!" I smiled and said, "That was Jessie. He was very sensitive to people and their feelings."

I am proud of the kind of person Jesse was

Jesse was working on a boat and getting it ready to go commercial fishing. He was fixing it up to do long line fishing. He had plenty of experience. For years, he was a deck hand for Stan Wood. Stan had a very successful fishery and flew his fish out, to the Lower 48.

Stan loved him. He said that when Jesse cleaned the fish, he never ever had to go back and check them. When he cleaned them *they were clean!* It was a difficult job with long hours, and Jesse would be buried in fish clear up past his waist all day long. He just kept cleaning those fish—all day and way into the next day, until the job was done. He never stopped! *Jesse would have done just fine back on the family farm!* Stan paid him really well, so to Jesse, it was worth it. He loved how independent he could be with all that money!

Another time, I had a job pulling in a power wire for a house. I asked Jesse to come and help me for an hour or two. He showed up and he had eight or nine guys with him, but that was the way it was with Jesse. We put in a ditch and pulled the wire through some walls and under the house. Everyone pitched in and helped. *Jesse was like the Pied Piper!*

It is going to be fantastic to see Jesse again one day. God has a perfect plan for all our suffering. The Holy Spirit shows and tells us astonishing things, to help us to survive, move forward, and get past unbearable things, like losing my son, Jesse.

When I go to the graveyard to be with Jesse, I know that his body is in that box, *but he is not in that box,* he is in Heaven, full of *life* in Jesus, and in a much better place. I have lived here in Haines over fifty years, and I have a lot of friends in the graveyard. *And then there's my son, Jesse.*

PRAYERS and MY CONDOLENCES

"I will never forget your precepts, for by them you have given me life."—Psalm 119:93

I know how it feels. Today, I pray for any of you who have lost a child—I'm so sorry. I pray each and every one of them is living eternal life with Jesus. In God, and in his loving spirit, we trust. Amen.

Hair, Hide, Guts and Feathers
June, 1963
Know Your Bears—in Camp and Out

Quote from *Lonesome Dove*:

Woodrow Call: [after handing the gun to Newt] "*It is better to have that and not need it, then to need it and not have it.*"

Alaska is bear country—they were here first and they know it. They are God's creation, but then again, so am I. More than once, I've had to protect myself from bears in the wild—they can run one hundred yards even after being shot in the heart. Truth is, coming upon bears, or being surprised by them happens in any deep woods country, camping or picnic areas up here. Even today, they are commonplace around Haines, and a great place to view bears. But beware, they are dangerous, especially for tourists who may not understand what to do, and what not to do—when to stand, when to run.

Black bears are one thing, but brown bears, the Grizzly's are another—you don't want to run into them in the woods on the trail—and the mama's—don't mess with any mama bear, no matter what kind she is—black or brown "Grizzly."

It goes without saying that we had bear problems in logging camp all the time. Every day, we covered the garbage from our meals, so thoroughly we used a D-6 Cat to do it. Even then, the bears would smell it and come and dig it up.

We knew we were one of the black bears favorite *café's*—they came into camp every night checking out the menu. Once in a while they would come in the daytime, but rarely.

We didn't have electricity in the logging camp, so we put cans of pop and milk in the creek to keep them cool. For a "refrigerator," for the other food, we used a garbage can, dug down into the water with only the lid sticking up out of the water. It worked fine because the water was cold, summer or winter. We cooked on a gas stove, taking turns cooking—they couldn't afford to hire cooks in those days. Since I liked to cook, I didn't mind pitching in, especially since some of the guys couldn't even boil water. It was a pretty simple kitchen arrangement, and the food wasn't bad.

Now back to the bears, the brown bears, Grizzly's, are the ones to watch out for—their tracks, *big tracks with claw imprints,* showed up in the dust of the road more often than we liked—it makes the hair stand up on the back of the neck of any sane person. Man, it gets the adrenalin flowing to run into one of those face-to-face!

One spring timber season in Alaska, we were falling timber on the mountain, with different people working at different places in the woods around the camp. It was pretty much uncharted territory; roads had to be built to get the timber out.

Two Canadian brothers were part of our crew. They were good timber fallers and had done it all their life. These two old-timers, both in their sixties, said they were falling a tree one day and one of them got his saw "dogged in" as they say. Wedged in like that, with the saw in the tree, man, it really makes noise! Hard on the ears! But above that intense loud sound, he heard an awful roar; no question, it was a grizzly bear. He, *or* probably she, was out there somewhere, but they couldn't see through the trees! Even this old-timer was shocked that this bear's roar drowned out the noise of the saw. Usually they take off when they get around people making this kind of stir in the forest.

The faller guessed that he was cutting down trees close to the bear's nest or den. *This bear was clearly upset!* The Canadian quickly got his brother, and even as a seasoned man of the woods, said, "Maybe we can chase that bear off with the saws!"

His brother said, "No! No! Not smart! That bear could slap the chainsaw clear out of your hands, you with it, and eat you for lunch!" Fortunately that didn't happen!

Lesson: Don't try to chase off a bear of any kind, especially a Grizzly, with a chainsaw or anything else. One swipe and you're out of business in more ways than one!

BEAR TIPS: 1) Try to avoid encounters with bears. *Of course!* **2)** Keep your distance; leave quietly and calmly, detour, do not disturb. **3)** If the bear is closer than 300 feet, *stand tall* and back away slowly. **4)** Know your bear. North America has three kinds of bears: brown bears, black bears, and polar bears. Grizzlies and black bears cannot necessarily be differentiated by their colors. Grizzly bears/brown bears can weigh up to and over 800 lbs., with a prominent shoulder hump and a rump lower than the shoulder. Black bears are typically smaller, up to 400 lbs. **5)** Understand a bears motivations—predatory (sees you as food) or protective (has cubs). **6)** Respond appropriately—See more complete advice on reputable websites about bears or at: www.wikihow.com/escape-from-a-bear/ where these brief recommendations are fully listed.

WILDLIFE (I invite you to visit: http://haines.ak.us/wildlife)

Nothing provides a thrill quite like seeing bears in the wild. Haines is home to both black and brown bears. Although bears can be seen virtually anywhere in the Chilkat Valley, certain areas are becoming well-known for optimal bear viewing opportunities. The Chilkoot River flows from Chilkoot Lake into Lutak Inlet and is one of the most easily reached bear viewing spots in Southeast Alaska from mid-June to October.

To minimize effects on wildlife habitat and make your bear viewing experiences safe and enjoyable for you, the bears, and all wildlife, stop by the visitor center for a Wildlife Viewing Guide and a check-list for Bear Safety. You may also visit the Alaska Fish and Game Wildlife Viewing site. (Information provided: Haines, Alaska listed above.)

The Hertz Family Crest

I love my family, past and present.—Erwin Hertz

Hertz—Herz family crest

Between the mid-17th to mid-20th centuries, German settlers arrived in America by the thousands. Poverty and religious persecution were great motivators in this large-scale migration. So too was the opportunity for tenant farmers to own their own land. The ancestral home of the Hertz family is in the German province of Bavaria . . . Austria and Russia—with some Jewish background. The Hertz name stands for a kindhearted and stalwart individual, and is derived from the German word "herz," which means "heart" (Ref. www.houseofnames.com)

I don't know exactly when my line of the Hertz family came to America. I wish I did. I do know that my grandfather *on my mother's side* was an officer in the German army in the First World War. He came to America after the war and settled in a German settlement in North Dakota. Since my father met my mother while living and farming in North Dakota, and they both preferred speaking German at home in my early years, I believe my father's family very likely came to America somewhere in that time-frame as well.

My brother, Clem, was back packing through Germany in the 70's, and he stopped in Frankfurt, Germany. He looked up the family crest for the Hertz family, the first one to find this out about the family. We do have the family crest. There is a book out on the Hertz family, as big as a telephone book, about one inch thick.

There are Hertz family reunions in different locations in the country. The Hertz family is listed as "builders" in the family crest information. It was spelled Herz, the German spelling, for Hertz.

But the plans of the LORD stand firm
forever, the purposes of his heart through
all generations.—Psalm 33:11

CHAPTER 12

GOD'S MIRACLES—
ALIVE AND REAL

"You are the God who performs miracles; you
display your power among the peoples."
—Psalm 77:14

People ask me, "What is your purpose in life?"
I tell them, "I want to go to heaven, and take as
many people with me as I can."
—Erwin Hertz

My Oldest Brother, Eugene, Saw an Angel—Glory to God!

"The sun will no more be your light by day, nor
will the brightness of the moon shine on you,
for the LORD will be your everlasting light, and
your God will be your glory."—Isaiah 60:19

I can pray, but I'm sure glad that God is in charge. My older brother,
Eugene, saw an angel a couple of years ago, on August 20, 2009.
It happened on the day my brother Richard died from Parkinson's
disease.

Richard battled the disease his way, his wife, Betty, always said, "He won't go to the doctor!" Instead, he kept on working on the dairy farm. I kind of chuckle about his Holstein cows—they were spoiled in the scheme of things. If they got fussy, Richard had a way of keeping them calm—he played music for them.

He still lived life, kept on with his work, but just walked and talked slower as he kept his dairy farm going. His herd of milk cows produced a high grade of milk for Darigold in Seattle—and he was even named Dairyman of the year once. That's prestigious for a dairy farmer! It all turned out okay for Richard, because staying active is one of the best things you can do for Parkinson's—and as everyone knows, dairy farming is really active—especially in the Hertz family!

A comical side note: Eugene and I helped him milk the cows when I was down from Alaska. The cows fought us when we tried to get them into their milking stations, they would not let their milk go, and then it would start squirting out of their bags, making a real mess. Slow but sure, we finally figured we had to do something different. There could only be one of us in the barn because they were confused by two strangers working there. We flipped a coin to see who had to milk the cows, and I lost! We were having a real rodeo trying to get those cows milked, but we did it, for Richard.

As I said earlier, I've met with a Promise Keepers group for years, every week at the Pioneer Bar here in Haines. (We always felt that was a good place to meet, because if customers wanted to come and pray with us they wouldn't feel out of place.)

At one meeting, I told Steve Vergen and Gene Strong, about my brother, Richard, and that I wanted to pray for him. I prayed that God's glory would be there with my brother when he died. I didn't know how God would do it, all I know is that God is faithful when we pray, and that he would answer my prayer for Richard to have a peaceful crossing over from this life when he died.

My youngest brother, Douglas, and I would pray together. He is the only brother that I pray with, anyway as I'm writing this book. Richard continued to struggle with the Parkinson's, and his system was beginning to shut down. He was having a tough time at the hospital. Finally, I felt we should have them take all his IV's and tubes out and let him die in peace. They were feeding him through a tube also, but even though he wasn't complaining he was hurting badly, I said to the family, "Just tell him to let go!"

Richard slept for about thirty hours after they disconnected him from everything. His wife and family were there, and my brother Eugene. He did not want Richard to go to sleep. I said, "What is the matter with you? He needs to sleep!" He was afraid that if he went to sleep that he wouldn't wake up.

When Richard did wake up, he asked, "Have the folks come to see me?" My dad had died ten years before, and my mom died fifteen years before Dad.

God is the only one that knows what we need, the perfect timing, the beginning and the end. But I continued to pray and ask, "God, please let your glory be with Richard when he dies." I didn't know if God was going to take him home, or give him more time. All I knew is that I wanted his glory to be there so that Richard would die in peace and have a peaceful crossing. Richard never did complain, he wanted to do things right, and for him quiet acceptance was the way to do chronic illness right. He was suffering in silence, but I trusted God to honor my prayers, in his way, in his time.

When Richard died I wasn't there, I was in Alaska, but the family was there, and stood all around his bed. When I talked to my brother, Eugene, he said there was a haze over my brother's body and bed, and an angel appeared. An angel came out of that haze, and he said, "Richard, I have come to take you to heaven with me!" My brother, Eugene, is the only one who saw and heard this—and I praise God, because I know my prayer was answered, Richard was in God's glory.

Eugene told me that when they opened the coffin at the funeral parlor, he told Richard's wife and the family about seeing the angel. It shocked everybody, because they didn't see anything when Richard died, even though Richard's wife was right beside him.

When I arrived a couple days later, Eugene did tell me, and said, "I thought I had lost my mind. I thought I'd gone off the deep end. I could not believe what I had seen and heard!" Eugene goes to church every Sunday, with a suit and tie on, goes through the motions, but he does not believe. To even admit what he had seen and heard was huge! He's never spoken about it to anyone again. I was so grateful, but in shock about what had happened. Even my two daughters said, "Now Dad that is a real miracle, your brother saying he saw an angel."

When I was in Alaska praying for God's glory for Richard, I never, ever, in a thousand years figured that God's glory would appear in that way. I am in awe of how God answers prayer.

I believe it happened because Eugene was the one that needed to see the angel, and by God's grace he did. Even though he told us this happened, to this day he still acts like he doesn't believe in God. I am praying for him. I gave him the book, *Beyond Death's Door,* but he says he can't read it. He has a history of heart attacks, and he is eighty years-old as I'm writing this book. We know that God has a perfect plan for all this, and I feel it will come to pass for him.

Eugene came up to Alaska to see me last year, and I asked him if he would go to church with me. I had told my friends that he was the one who had seen the angel, and he said, "No! Please don't do that!" He still isn't comfortable with it yet! He hasn't even told his children. I guess they'll know if they read this book!

But God is in charge! I am glad that I can pray and that I am not in charge of anything! Thank you Lord, hallelujah!

"Rodger, God is Merciful!"

> "He performs wonders that cannot be fathomed,
> miracles that cannot be counted."—Job 5:9

To be thankful is one of the most important capacities of the human mind. As we practice it carefully and constantly we develop a deep joy in living even though life is filled with all kinds of suffering and difficulty. The individual who learns to practice daily thanksgiving, will surround himself with continuous victories and increase his blessings from God—to experience days filled with victory, joy, and satisfaction. It is important to remember that we will contribute to the happiness of all those that touch our lives when we live a life of faith and thankfulness. Praise God!

I'm thankful to have opportunities to meet all kinds of people, and sometimes have a chance to touch their lives for God. Rodger was not a close friend, but someone I used to play gold medal basketball with him when we were young men—I played for the Skagway Railroad and he played for the Pioneer Bar in Haines, Alaska.

We were all full of spunk and vigor, doing whatever came down the road in Alaska, with work and play, like young men do. Before long, he left Haines, and got married, and I got married, too. Then, about twenty-five to thirty years after he had left Haines, he came back and was driving a taxi cab. Yes, we have lots of tourists, so we do have taxi cabs. (Chuckle)

I saw him in town after hearing that he had terminal cancer, but hadn't had a chance to talk to him. I told the Promise Keepers that I wanted to pray for him, and then go talk with him to see if we could help him—we prayed and then I went to see him. He was staying with a man in town, and I went to the house. We talked some.

He said "What are you doing?"

I told him. "Well, I belong to a group called Promise Keepers, and we are praying for you because I heard that you have terminal cancer."

He was very upfront about it. "That's right; they told me I haven't got long to live."

I decided to be straightforward. "Rodger, we prayed together for you today, and I came here to talk to you. I'd like to pray with you, too."

Abruptly, he said "I don't believe in any of that crap!"

I smiled at him. "I know, Rodger. That's exactly why I came here today!"

We talked for a while longer, and he told me that they were going to do some experimental treatment on him in Seattle. I told him more about our prayers, Jesus, and God. He insisted that he didn't believe in any of it. I replied with, "Well, I would like to keep talking to you if you don't mind, and I would like to come over a few times and talk to you before you leave for Seattle".

I went back to Promise Keepers the next week, and we prayed that he would let me keep talking and praying with him.

I went to see him again, and Rodger said, "I was married three times, and I was a terrible husband and father. My kids are all messed up and on drugs, because I wasn't a good father."

I decided to tell him about my logging accident, and what God had done for me. "When I was working in the woods, I was hit by a tree, dead, I'm sure, but God saw fit to give me more time on this earth. I had an out-of-body experience, looking down on my body on the ground—it changed me forever. And I went on to tell him, I'm no stranger to problems of all kinds."

We kept talking. "Rodger, when a near death spiritual experience like that happens to you, it changes a person. I didn't think I was changed, but I soon began to understand the changes happening within me. I'll never be perfect. I'll always have a lot of growing to do, but I am different in a good way."

His comment back to me, "I just want to die and get to hell out of here!"

I couldn't leave that alone. "Roger, you will go to another place; it doesn't stop here!"

He didn't believe my logging experience, but I spoke the truth as I know it. "It's real. Rodger, it's more real than us talking right now. You have a choice before you go, you can go to heaven or go to hell! If I were you, I would want to go to heaven!"

Rodger said it again. "I just don't believe in that crap! Besides, I have been such a rotten person all my life; my marriages, my children being all messed up, I just want to get out of here and get it over with!"

I told him that some years after God saw fit to give me more time on this earth, after the logging accident, I finally found this book, *Beyond Death's Door.* I asked him if he would read the book, and he said "No, that experience you had happened to you, not to me!"

So I shared that I would like to keep praying and coming to talk to him, because, "Rodger, being saved is for everybody! Ten years after that happened to me, I read in "Reader's Digest" about a guy who told about being dead, and looking at his body after he had crossed over to the other side. That is where I was Rodger! And it was amazing what happened for the brief time I was there. I was so peaceful and a feeling of being in the presence of something really beautiful. I had complete confidence, peace, love and joy. It felt so unbelievably good, I did not want to come back to earth, which was odd since I had only been married a short time, and Georgia was eight months pregnant. We were very much in love and we were just starting out. Rodger, you have a choice, you just have to make it; it is not that hard." Then I prayed with Rodger.

He seemed to mellow a bit. "Well, why don't you come back again and we can talk some more?"

The guys at Promise Keeper were excited about the small change of attitude as I kept praying with Rodger, and the fact that Rodger finally stopped saying "I don't believe in that crap!" I went back several times to talk with him, we all kept praying for him as he got ready to go to Seattle. He asked if I would call him when he got down to Seattle.

"Sure, when you get settled in the hospital, and wherever you're staying, let me know." He called, and our Promise Keepers started in again praying where we left off. It was amazing to begin seeing the work God was doing in Rodger's life—he was starting to see there was a choice he could make, between heaven and hell.

I explained more about Jesus. "Rodger, to believe, receive the Lord, Jesus Christ, and all he has done for you. Jesus died on the cross for your sins, and for my sins. God, his father, raised him from the dead. He made that sacrifice, died on the cross, to provide us, everybody who calls on him, a way to forgiveness and acceptance with God, in heaven."

It was getting really interesting, even though Rodger kept saying, "There is no hope for me. I am a terrible sinner, terrible father, terrible husband, terrible everything! I am a really rotten person."

I told him "It doesn't matter, Rodger, we are all sinners. None of us are without sin." I told him about the part of my journey with Promise Keepers. Also, "I am Catholic and I have always gone to church, have always gone to confession. It has helped me learn more about God all of my life, or I wouldn't even be here talking to you, Roger."

He kept on with his treatments, different kinds of chemo-radiation, and he got so sick. He was staying by himself, living in an apartment by the hospital, but he got confused and accidently overdosed. They pumped out his stomach and he survived that, but he wasn't doing well.

I kept phoning, and praying for him. One day he asked Jesus to come into his heart. He said to me, "I believe in Jesus Christ." I told him how happy it made me and the guys at Promise Keepers. He was getting close to the end, and I didn't know. Some months went by since he'd gone to Seattle, and I kept praying with him once a week.

The last time I talked to him, I didn't know it was going to be the last. I'm thankful that I said, "When Jesus was on the cross, there were two criminals, one on each side of Jesus." I said, "Rodger, you are on the cross with Jesus right now. You are going to die and you know it. Jesus was on the cross and he knew he was going to die, too."

One of the thieves hanging beside him said, "If you are Jesus get us off these crosses and get us out of here!"

And the other thief said "Don't you fear God, since you are close to death?" He asked Jesus if he would remember him when he came into his kingdom. Jesus told him "Today you will be with me in paradise!" I said, "Rodger you are close to death right now! You are going to die and you know it. All you have to do is ask Jesus if you will be in paradise with him when you die. It is not that hard Rodger, just do it. Acknowledge what Jesus did for you. Just give everything to God . . . and let go!" He did.

I did not know that was the last time I was going to talk to him, but it was.

Luke 23:39-43

Then one of the criminals who were hanged blasphemed him, saying, "If you are the Christ, save yourself and us."

But the other, answering, rebuked him, saying, "Do you not even fear God, seeing you are under the same condemnation?

And we indeed justly, for we receive the due reward of our deeds; but this man has done nothing wrong."

Then he said to Jesus, "Lord, remember me when you come into Your kingdom."

And Jesus said to him, "Assuredly, I say to you, today you will be with me in Paradise."

The next time I called, a lady answered the phone, and I asked, "Do I have the wrong number? I'm calling for Rodger."

She said "No, this is the right number. He died at four a.m. this morning. I am his daughter."

Rodger had told me about her, and that she was all mixed up because of all the drugs he did and she did. I said "Was Rodger okay . . . at peace, before he died?"

She said she had talked with him before he died. "He told me not to worry about him, because he believed in Jesus Christ!"

All I could say to her was, "Wow!" It was God's amazing grace once again.

Apparently, while he was having treatment in Seattle, he went to see his former wife, some of his children, and cousins. His daughter told me she had asked them to forgive him and he asked if he could help them. He tried to give them some money or whatever he had left. Everyone was very surprised about how much he had changed.

They did not know it was me that had been talking to Rodger about God. Then I told her the story. She said, "You were the one!"

"The one what?"

"You're the one who prayed with him!"

Yes, but I couldn't take the credit. "There were a bunch of us praying for him! The Promise Keepers group in Haines—we all prayed for him. I can't take responsibility and reward for that. I was just one of many—we put him on different prayer chains, too.

It was a powerful work God did in Rodger—the rest of us aren't anybody without Jesus; we were just obedient to pray. I thank the Lord for his faithfulness. This event, with Rodger, is real-life evidence of the power of God, and the love of Jesus Christ, and the Holy Spirit's intervention for a desperate man. No one is too far gone to receive all God offers. Are you a person who feels you are too far gone? Or maybe someone else comes to mind that you can pray for—either way, it's never too late.

Don't give up on yourself or any other person, pray instead. God hears you.

WE NEED GOD'S HAND ON US

Have mercy on us. Fill us with your grace and your protection. I plead the blood of Jesus over me, my family and all others that I pray for.

Thank you, Lord, for restoring your blessing on me with each sunrise, and the confidence that I, and others who know you, are redeemed by the blood of Jesus, each and every day.

Thank you Lord, God. You said that you would never leave or forsake us. Thank you Lord Jesus, for your sacrifice for us on the cross, and that you draw us up to you, closer and closer.

Thank you Lord Jesus, every day you are faithful when we ask for fresh faith in our life, and for your guidance in our life—until the day you come to take us home to heaven. I pray this for me, my family—and for those who receive you, and are of the family of God. Amen.

Haines Boy's Basketball Team—Alaska State Champions 2010

> "Therefore the Lord, the God of Israel, declares: 'I
> promised that members of your family would minister
> before me forever.' But now the Lord declares: 'Far be it
> from me! Those who honor me I will honor, but those
> who despise me will be disdained."
> —1 Samuel 2:30

> I pray for a clean heart today, Lord; a clean mind and
> clean strong body to serve you every day and every night
> of my life. We need, and I need, your hand on us every
> day and night of our life.
> —Erwin Hertz

Everything is worthy of prayer, even basketball.

The Southeast Tournament is Region Five, in Alaska. I was walking down the hallway at the high school and came across, Kyle Fossman, our champion basketball player at the time in Haines. He had on a dress shirt and tie.

"Hi, Kyle; what's going on?"

He said, "We have the playoff game here this weekend to see who will play in the final championship game in Sitka." They had to beat Sitka to be able to compete in the final championships. We talked for a little bit and he left for class. As he walked away, a voice said, "Pray for him!" I looked around, but there was no one there but me, and Kyle walking away. I recognized that it was the Lord. I said, "Ok, Lord, I will pray, and I will have the prayer chain pray, too."

Right away I wondered what the connection was. I knew his grandfather, Cliff Fossman, and remembered a story he had told me years before. His wife, Dorothy, was dying of cancer at the time, and being treated in the hospital in Seattle. She got weaker and weaker and was in a wheelchair. A priest showed up to visit, since she did not have much longer.

Now Cliff was an old Navy man, and he kind of laughed when he said this, but I guess the priest only weighed about ninety pounds in a wet pea coat—apparently he was a very small man! Clifford was with her every day, and so was the priest; he went everywhere with them. The priest just loved Dorothy. He prayed with her and hugged her every day—and Clifford felt that God had sent the priest, as if he was an angel to help Dorothy to cross over to the other side, to be with God in Heaven.

Cliff had never talked about dying and going to heaven; it was not in his vocabulary, yet he told me this story that honored God—when Dorothy died, the priest was there to help Dorothy cross over to the other side.

I was amazed, because the Bible tells us in 1 Samuel 2:30, when you honor God, God honors you. God asked me or us to pray for Kyle, so I would honor God by praying for Kyle Fossman, a third generation in the Fossman family.

With this in mind, I went to the basketball game at the high school that night, February 19th, and I prayed differently. Rather than pray for the team, then go watch the game, that night I prayed non-stop for Kyle throughout the whole game. His dad, Steve Fossman, was the coach. I felt the peace of my prayers being answered as people sat all around me. It was really a tight, hard fought, game. I think it even went into over-time, but Haines won, and the series, so they were eligible to go play at the regional games in Sitka, March 4th and 5th.

The players were gearing up for the regional games at Sitka, and I was at the bank one day and told some of them that we would be praying for the Haines players. The game would be on the radio. They played Metlakatla on the first night, March 4th, and the next night, March 5th, they played Mt. Edgecomb for the Southeast Championship.

I listened to the game where I would not be interrupted. Boy, those games were close, full of fouls; very intense. I was so proud of our players; they were giving it all they had. In the final Regional Championship game on the 5th, throughout the game the announcer from Sitka kept saying, "They have got to stop Fossman! They have to stop Fossman!" As I listened to it on the radio, I was on my knees praying! I had to—there was no stopping! They were that close.

Kyle Fossman just kept on giving it his all, as did all the players. They were focused, and each played powerful and passionate in the final playoff games. Kyle Fossman was the catalyst, but I give credit to Steve as the coach, and his wife, Anne Marie, and his mother. The ladies traveled to out-of-town games with the team—the three of them always kept the boys with them, made sure they ate right, went to bed on time, talked strategy and everything. I was so impressed with how they handled the responsibilities of coaching and traveling with the team! I give them credit; it made a huge difference in their winning the Southeast Championship, and eventually the State Championship.

I went to the basketball games at the high school in Haines, but I hadn't followed the games as much since my kids were grown and gone. The 2010 team came back to Haines from the regional championship, to a town that was really impressed and proud.

The players left for the State Championship in Anchorage at the Sullivan Arena, on March 15-17. March 15, they played Galena. Then March 16th, they played Point Barrow. Winning both, then they played the final State Championship game against Nome, March 17th.

That was a whole different ball game. Haines had won some games against Nome before this, so they were really going after Haines this time! Plus, there was a state championship up for grabs. It was on TV here in Haines. I went to Terry Sharnbrois house, the same place I'd gone in the regional playoffs—again, praying on my knees the whole time. I couldn't stop, it was that close.

Terry and I are good friends who have prayed together for years—for logging contests and games. We were used to praying together, but Terry was pacing up and down in the kitchen like a cougar in a cage. I said, "Terry, stop. You've got to pray!" He said, "I can't stand it, it is so much pressure!"

Man, like most playoffs, the last game was close. The gym was in an up-roar. We could hear it all on TV. Except for our small town, everybody else up there thought Haines would get beat! I was almost on my face praying, because Haines was behind the last few seconds of the game. Then Kyle stole the ball from the guy who was dribbling down to the basket at full speed—Kyle, also running full-speed, took that ball! I don't know how he got it without fouling, but he did.

Time out! It stopped the game when Kyle got the ball—the Nome coaches and kids were in shock! Back in play, Kyle stole the ball again! Haines was ahead at that point, but if the Nome player could have made a basket, it would have been Nome's game. I was more than amazed that Kyle could do that twice. Our little town won the State Basketball Championship. Steve, Ann Marie and Kyle, got off the ferry, and came over to me and said, "It worked, it worked, it worked! The prayers worked!"

As I prayed, as we all prayed, I felt confirmation. God does not give second place! We had a party at Steve and Ann Marie's and they had a recording that we watched again. Kyle is an extremely talented and focused player—very mature, plus a fantastic young man. I told him that I would be glad to pray for him any time of day or night. He has an great career ahead of him.

God does not want sacrifice, he wants obedience! He wants you to listen, and when he tells you to pray, he answers. He wants us to pray when we feel him nudge us to do so. We must listen and pay attention, and pray confidently. He will take care of everything else! Like Kyle and the players on that team, we have to be focused in prayer—have good intent, and give thanks and praise as we do so. I'm glad God got my attention in the high school hallway—and that I listened.

Haines, our little town in southeast Alaska was the State Basketball Champion in 2010. *Some might call it a miracle—once again, for me, God confirmed he answers prayers of every kind!*

In Jesus Name, I Rebuke . . .

> "She kept this up for many days. Finally Paul became so
> annoyed that he turned around and said to the spirit, 'In
> the name of Jesus Christ I command you to come out of
> her!' At that moment the spirit left her."
> —Acts 16:18

One morning I was working on an electrical job at the high
school. There was a problem with the fire alarm—as always, I said
my prayers as I went to work on this complicated system. I had
been working less than an hour when, suddenly, I saw a vision. It
was an image of a teenage girl I knew, Jessica. She was a rare jewel
in life, and a girl I knew to have strong faith. I could see that she
was dressed in a green sweater and jeans—and that she was standing
in front of a man with beard. In my mind and in my spirit, I knew
Jessica was standing in front of Jesus. She was not here, but over
on the other side, with him in the spirit. To be honest, this vision
scared me! I didn't fully understand, nor feel worthy. I needed to
kneel in prayer and seek God's calming reassurance.

> **"I, Daniel, was troubled in spirit, and the visions that
> passed through my mind disturbed me."**
> —Daniel 7:15

I left the building, and went out to the alley to my truck. I knelt
down and prayed by the truck until I felt God's peace return. I went
back into the school and got right back to work on the fire alarm
system. I had been working about an hour when John Marquardt
came through the back door of the school. (John is the father of
Jessica.) I could tell he had been crying. I asked, "What's happening
John, what's the matter?"

He was really upset. "Did you know that Jessica was killed this
morning?"

I told him I'd seen her, what had happened earlier, and explained what I had seen. I described the clothes Jessica was wearing—and the vision of seeing her with Jesus.

"It's unbelievable." he said. "That is exactly what she was wearing." He and I have know each other for years, and are often on the same page—he understood and accepted that God had allowed me to see Jessica.

Distressed myself, I quietly said again, "Yes. I saw her standing in front of Jesus." We both cried.

Unfortunately, she had fallen asleep while driving and died at the scene. She left this world that morning, and was in the spirit—I saw her; Jessica with Jesus. I know God gives simple men visions, like in Acts 9:12 (In a vision he has seen a man named Ananias come and place his hands on him to restore his sight . . .), but I didn't know why God had given me this glimpse of heaven.

I talked to John a few more times over the next few days, before the funeral. I knew the priest who officiated, Father Mike Schwarte. It goes without saying it was a very hard and emotional time. John's wife, Geraldine, normally a very excitable person, was unusually calm at the funeral.

John's family lived in a house thirty miles out of town, so after the service and burial, I decided to go out to their house with this dedicated young priest, Father Mike. We wanted to see if they were doing alright. We stopped at Jessica's gravesite and prayed over it. We talked and prayed more as we drove to their house. It had been a few hours since the service—we were uneasy and feeling a strong need to go out there. By now it was dark.

As we drove up, we saw someone walking up and down in the yard. It was John, obviously terribly distressed. We got out of the car and could hear awful screaming coming from inside the house. John told us that Gerri was in agony, unlike anything he had ever seen.

She had completely unraveled after the funeral and she wanted to commit suicide. For three hours he had tried everything he knew to do (even cold water), but nothing helped to snap her out of it or calm her.

When we opened the door to the house, it was like opening the door to hell! I'm sorry, but there is no other way to describe it. The older kids were trying to hold her and keep her under control. The younger kids were crying, and she was screaming like a mad woman—she intended to kill herself. We walked right into her horrible torment when we entered.

She was not that physically strong of a woman, but the demons within her were. I knew the outcome of such a horrendous scene, but also knew God was in charge. When I was in high school they took us on a field trip, and we toured an insane asylum—I suppose today it is called a mental institution. The nurses' station was ten feet square and protected from the four hundred women who all seemed to be screaming at the same time.

I had never seen or heard anything like those women screaming until I walked into John's house that dark night—not only dark because it was night, but inside the house, and inside this woman, oppression of spiritual darkness existed. I prayed to the Lord. "Be gone Satan, you have no power or authority on earth—you were defeated over two thousand years ago when Jesus died on the cross." I had to declare the need for protection in the name of Jesus. I claimed it with confidence as we approached Gerri who was screaming and kicking. (We all must learn to stand firm in Jesus Christ when we face spiritual warfare.)

We knew there was no talking to her, she was way past that. However, Father Mike said to her, "I love you." Today, Gerri remembers the immediate sense of hope those words brought to her in that terrible time of bondage. We prayed as we held her down; we kept her from hurting herself.

We began to pray and *praise God, praise the Lord Jesus* and *praise the Holy Spirit*—against the tyranny of demons that made her strong. Father Mike added, "*Come* Holy Spirit." It was a battle. She tried to get away for nearly an hour—I looked into her eyes and could see the madness that controlled her.

As I write this, I am praying to be covered, (me and my family) with the blood of Jesus. I pray the covering and protection of the sweet blood of Jesus for all who read this. Always praise the Lord

Jesus who has all authority to cast out demons. In Jesus name, we are able to overcome—and able to help others do the same.

> **"When Jesus had called the Twelve together, he gave them power and authority to drive out all demons and to cure diseases . . ."**
> Luke 9:1

I was about to learn a lot about spiritual battles from this one experience. I asked Gerri if she would sit down with us if we let go of her. We were holding on to her in the upstairs hallway. She said that she would if I would do an exorcism on her. I thought about it. I had never done one before, but had read about them, and been taught what to do. It was a serious matter that could only be dealt with by calling on God's power, his word and trusting in the Holy Spirit to do what is impossible for man. In Jesus Christ we have the authority, but we have to be willing to step up to the plate, step into the battlefield of spiritual warfare. It can be hard, it can feel scary. (See: Matthew 8: 28-34) Father Mike admitted to me later that he was a split second from running away, down the road, when he entered that house. It was frightening to see Gerri in such a struggle.

> **"Call on me in the day of trouble; I will deliver you, and you will honor me."**
> —Psalm 50:15

In Jesus holy name, I rebuked the demons in Gerri, and in Jesus' authority cast them out. I prayed, I praised—Father Mike prayed and praised! The Holy Spirit came into the house—*powerfully!*

Peace, as only God can provide through his power and might—his mercy brought calm to the chaos within Gerri's soul. I looked into her eyes and I could see Gerri again, not the demons that had overtaken her.

> "But I have raised you up for this very purpose, that I
> might show you my power and that my name might be
> proclaimed in all the earth."
> —Exodus 9:16

The kids started jumping up and down—they could feel the peace brought forth by the Holy Spirit. We stayed there for awhile to make sure everything was okay. A scene like that leaves a person feeling totally wiped out. But somehow when we entered that house I knew what we were walking into. God provided us the means to overcome. Only in Jesus could we do anything, and thankfully we did—*he did!*

I couldn't sleep, and neither could Father Mike. Together we walked up and down the hill by my house praising the Lord. It was bitter cold outside, but I was so happy to see how God had released Gerri from such torment that I didn't feel it! As we walked and praised Jesus, we reminded each other to remember to pray to be covered in the blood of Jesus, for our own protection, any time before doing spiritual battle. We had not remembered to do it in their house that night, but still God was faithful to protect us.

> "God has delivered [her] from going down to the pit,
> [she] shall live to enjoy the light of life."
> —Job 33:28

Lord, I praise you again and again. You will never forsake us. (Neh. 9:31; Heb. 13:5)

> "Praise be to the LORD God, the God of Israel, who
> alone does marvelous deeds."
> —Psalm 72:18

Amen *and* Amen!

After a few days, Ari (Ariana), Jessica's three-year-old sister went by herself out to Jessica's room. It was outside the main part of the house. Simply put, she saw Jessica. (That's what she said, and little kids don't usually make up such things.)

She ran to tell the rest of the kids—Sarah, Daniel, Nicholas, Luke, Adam, and Jeddiah. When they went back out to Jessica's room with Ari, they discovered this poem in an otherwise empty journal, lying on her bed with a pen beside it.

I include this poem in remembrance of Jessica—for John, Gerri, and Jessica's sisters and brothers.

Do Not Stand at My Grave and Weep

Written by Mary Elizabeth Frye, 1932

Do not stand at my grave and weep

I am not there. I do not sleep.

I am a thousand winds that blow.

I am the diamond glints on snow.

I am the sunlight on ripened grain.

I am the gentle autumn rain.

When you awaken in the morning's hush

I am the swift uplifting rush

Of quiet birds in circled flight.

I am the soft stars that shine at night.

Do not stand at my grave and cry;

I am not there. I did not die.

Kidneys Can be a Pain

> And he said: "The Lord is my rock and my
> fortress and my deliverer; the God of my strength,
> in whom I will trust . . ."
> —2 Samuel 22:2-3

God had put it on my heart to start a prayer chain, but I hadn't done it yet. For some reason, I was unsure and intimidated about doing it, even though I was part of other prayer chains. I felt compelled to tell the Lord something *I thought* he might not know. "Lord, if I tell them at church that I want to be in charge of starting a new prayer chain, they will laugh me out of church!"

I had, and still have, kidney problems. What does the prayer chain have to do with my kidneys? I'll tell you. Some years ago, I went to Missoula, Montana, where my brother, Eugene, lived to see what was up with them—I knew something was wrong. I drank a lot of water, and I once met a doctor that told me to eat a whole watermelon once-in-a-while. Now that can be a chore, but I do it sometimes!

Now that I was older, I had kidney stone attacks, but headed to a specialist in Missoula to have more tests. He x-rayed my kidneys and said, "You have something wrong with your kidneys."

"Uh, yeah . . ."

He told me he wanted to do more testing, but I was feeling pretty good, and I didn't hear back from him. Since no one called, I decided to go back to Alaska. I figured that I could do more in Juneau if it was needed, so scheduled a flight home. (I've had three brothers with cancer, but I live pretty healthy and drink Essiac Tea, and in my opinion, it is a detoxification that is good to fight cancer.)

While I was waiting to catch the plane back to Alaska, Eugene came back out to the airport. (Before cell phones and high airport security) He told me the hospital had called, and they wanted me to come back.

I agreed, but it wasn't good news. The doctor's concern, "You have a spot, about as big as a quarter, on your left kidney and it is serious. I'm suspicious of cancer for several reasons." He went on to explain.

The next morning, I went back into the hospital the next morning to have a biopsy of the kidney.

When Eugene took me to the doctor that morning, he panicked and said, "You'll have to take chemo! If you have cancer, you'll have to take chemo!"

With my usual conviction, I said, "What are you talking about? I am never, ever going to take chemo, even if I have leprosy, or whatever, I am not taking chemo! I have my own theory about chemo!"

I have lost many friends to cancer, and they were doing really well until they took chemo. I know that is a generalized statement to make, because some people are helped, but I would not choose to take chemo myself—in my mind, it's just not an option.

It was bright and early, and the nurse began prepping me. The doctor and the whole crew were there, ready to go ahead with the biopsy. It took about an hour to do this and that, and get all the IV's set. I guess if I had a reaction when they put the dye into my body, they could start my heart again using one of those IV's!

I had the book, *The Purpose Driven Life* with me, and the nurse said, "We did a Bible Study on that book. I'm finished, and they will come and get you pretty soon. Do you want anything—bathroom, blankets—anything at all before they come to get you?"

I replied, "No, I'm fine. But I do want you to pray with me if you would."

She said, "Ok, what do you want to pray?"

"I want to pray that when I go in the operating room that they will not find anything!"

She kind of frowned and said, "Well, they have already found it!"

"I know! I saw it on the x-rays the doctor showed me." . . . we prayed!

In the operating room, they had extra doctors and people on hand waiting in case they had to do something more radical than a biopsy. I went in after praying with the nurse, and the doctor started putting the dye in.

I could tell the doctor was getting pretty shook up. Something wasn't going quite right. He was an expert in his field, and a good doctor—and I had seen the spot too. But God said, "My people don't ask, ask and you shall receive!"

"So Judah gathered together to ask help from the Lord; and from all the cities of Judah they came to seek the Lord."—2 Chronicles 20:4

It was a little like an amusement park ride after I was wheeled in to the surgical area—the doctors turned me every-which-way, putting dye into me, and whatever else was needed—everything but stand me on my head. As time went on, I started smiling—they could not find the spot on my kidney! I said, "Thank you, Lord!" All I had done was asked—to be healed!

The doctor was a bit upset! The anesthesiologist sat there with his chin on his hand, waiting to put me to sleep. But it wasn't looking like the doctor was going to need to go in and take the biopsy. They didn't find anything! I said, "Wow! Wow! Wow! Those two important words popped into my head and heart again; **life** and **amen!** He probably thought I was a bumbling idiot, but what else could I say, but wow . . . ?"

As I walked out of the hospital that day, I smiled again, agreeing with what the Lord had placed on my heart. "Ok, Lord, you got me! I will start the prayer chain! I'm listening; yes, I will start the prayer chain!"

When I got home, I told everyone at church what had happened in the hospital, and that I wanted to start a prayer chain. I had six women that signed up right away, and I said to them, "This is not a gossip chain! This is a prayer chain!" . . . not to pick on you women, but I feel it's important to remember. Today, our prayer chain is still going strong!

Praise God—Praise the Lord Jesus—
Praise the Holy Spirit

> . . . so that at the name of Jesus every knee will bow,
> of those who are in heaven and on earth
> and under the earth . . .
> —Philippians 2:10

> I believe anything is possible when we
> call on the name of Jesus!
> —Erwin Hertz

Clyde Bell, now passed, was a man in Haines I prayed for, and with, many times. He had a lot of addictions he could not overcome, and he had plenty of problems. Actually, we had a pretty good relationship despite it all. Obviously with his lifestyle and health challenges he was under attack a lot. I tried to be there for him, and coach him through it, when he welcomed my support.

Some years had gone by since we gotten together to pray—for awhile he had chosen not to pray anymore. Now, his health was failing and he didn't have long to live.

He stopped at my house one morning, and he shared that he was not doing well at all. I told him, "Clyde, you are under attack. You need to protect yourself. God can help you!"

I had told him this many times before, but since it had been awhile I told him again, "When you are under attack, whether it is fear, shame, guilt, regret, depression, anxiety; overcome in dark and negative thoughts, Clyde, all you have to do is praise God, praise the Lord Jesus, praise the Holy Spirit! That is all you have to do; say that and mean it! Satan will leave you alone because he can't stand the name of God, Jesus or the Holy Spirit. He goes away! He leaves!"

I said it again, "Whenever you feel under attack, say that phrase! If you can't remember it, just say, 'Lord Jesus, please help me!' That is all you have to do, Clyde."

"If you can't remember Jesus, please save me—just call out the name, Jesus! It is tried and true; it is the word of God! I use it all the time, but I know you don't feel like hearing all my stories." I knew he was failing fast, and he did die a few days later—I didn't know he was so close to death.

My next door neighbor, Kathy, was good friends with Clyde, and I prayed with her sometimes, too. They had a party, not a funeral for Clyde.

A few days after the "funeral party," I was driving home from work, and Kathy was trying to get my attention—she was waving like crazy; jumping up and down. I had no idea what was going on. I quickly parked in my carport and walked over to see her in the yard.

She was so excited. She said, "I saw Clyde, I saw Clyde!"

"Really, when was that?" I questioned.

Without pausing, she said "I saw him this morning!"

"How did you know it was him? He is dead! What did he say?"

She was absolute, but couldn't remember everything. "He said praise something, praise something, praise something!"

I was in awe. "Really?"

She went on, "I couldn't understand what he said other than that!"

I asked her, "Did he say praise God; praise the Lord Jesus; praise the Holy Spirit?"

Smiling, Kathy exclaimed, "Yes! Yes! Yes! That is exactly what he said!"

"Wow!" I couldn't get over it. God is so amazing in how he works in people's lives. I explained to Kathy about the power of praising God, Jesus and the Holy Spirit for all kinds of reasons, but especially when under attack from the enemy. And I told her how I had shared that with Clyde, and prayed for him to understand and act on it.

I believe what Kathy told me, because I hadn't told her, or anyone else, what I had said to Clyde. Only Clyde knew, and I firmly believe he called on God, Jesus, and the Holy Spirit—due to God's amazing grace, Clyde is saved, and praising God with the angels in heaven. I am so thankful Clyde listened. Acceptance and surrender; Christ's blood; power of prayer—and the divine purpose of God—*all are keys to eternity!*

Overcoming Darkness

> . . . His lamp shone over my head, and by
> His light I walked through darkness; . . .
> —Job 29:3

> I had never felt or experienced
> anything like this in my life.
> —Erwin Hertz

To this point in my life, as I write this book, my divorce has been the most difficult time I've ever experienced—a time of disappointment in myself, wishing I'd done some things differently—I've had challenges and adjustments, and felt sadness and uncertainty.

This strange occurrence happened after my divorce—during a tough time. No doubt I was in an exposed, sad and vulnerable state. I was a prime target for attack from the enemy through fear, lack of God's peace, self-condemnation, and other things that kept me off balance, and can interrupt a close walk with God.

It was morning, but it was still dark in the bedroom as I began to wake up. The sun was barely beginning to rise, so it wasn't light, yet it wasn't dark either. My bedroom has a large window the full length of the bedroom. I was sleeping next to the window on that side of the bed. I can't say I was totally awake, but I wasn't asleep—you know that half awake feeling. But without a doubt I knew there was something in the corner of my bedroom. My back was to the window, and there was a dark form in that corner of the bedroom—my back was to it, still, I knew the form was there! I knew what it was, and it definitely was not a good thing.

Because of my relationship with Jesus Christ, I innately knew it was some sort of dark spirit; like Satan. It represented the dark side, darkness of the world. I was not afraid—and because of Jesus, I had confidence and knowledge that in Christ, the outcome would be okay, but still, what was going to happen?

> **"For we do not wrestle against flesh and blood, but against principalities, against powers, against the rulers of the darkness of this age, against spiritual hosts of wickedness in the heavenly places."**
> —Ephesians 6:12

I'm only human, so I can't fully explain it, but very slowly, this silent force got more menacing, darker and bigger. I knew it was there, and I knew it was threatening, and had evil plans and intentions for me. Whatever it was moved towards the bed and I didn't make a move. I didn't say anything. I continued to just lay there, not asleep and not awake. I felt this dark mass was going to try to harm me. This thing came over by the bed, and got right up to where I was laying on my side, near my shoulder beside the bed. Still, without moving, I just waited to see what was going to happen.

I sensed there was a being there in that dark mass! My back was to whatever it was. I don't know if it knelt down or what, but it felt like an arm went underneath my shoulder, around my neck, and a forearm pressed down across my throat. The arm grabbed the free arm, and had my neck in scissors, holding my neck in a tight grip. The apex of two arms came across my throat directly on my Adam's apple. It wasn't happening fast, just kind of slow.

Slowly, I felt more pressure pushing down hard on my throat—it got more and more severe, more forceful. I just started praising the Lord; I said, "Praise God, praise Lord Jesus, praise the Holy Spirit," over and over again! That is all I did.

At the point where I felt my throat was being crushed is when I said the words that are above all—and as soon as I started speaking and praising God out loud, that whole thing just dissolved. Not fast and not slow, but it went away a lot quicker than it came, because it came very slowly. Soon, I could feel it completely disappear from me and the room! I already knew what the outcome would be as I praised Jesus, but I didn't know what the dark force was, other than it wanted to do harm in my life, not good, something to disrupt my life.

Since that time, I have never been attacked exactly like that again (praise God). But it is important to share so we all know and remember the power provided, in God, Jesus Christ, and the Holy Spirit, against the evil one—we need not fear; God is ever-present with us. For He Himself has said, "I will never leave you nor forsake you."—Hebrews 13:5.

Another verse to commit to your heart and mind: "Do not fear, for I am with you; do not anxiously look about you, for I am your God. I will strengthen you, surely I will help you, Surely I will uphold you with my righteous right hand." Isaiah 41:10 (NASB)

MY PRAYER—BEGIN EACH DAY IN THE FULL ARMOR OF GOD

"Heavenly Father, I desire to be obedient by being strong in the Lord and the power of your might. I recognize that it is essential to put on the armor that you have provided. I do so now with gratitude, praise, and in faith in you, as effective spiritual protection against the spiritual forces of darkness."—Ephesians 6:10-18

I pray these verses with 'the blood of Jesus.' Amen!

A Lifetime of God's Miracles

Sold Out for Jesus, Lock, Stock and Barrel

I thank God for the miracles I have experienced and witnessed. I've shared several earlier in this chapter, and others throughout this book. He has given love, joy and peace to me in spades! I am sold out for Jesus and I want you to be, too!—Erwin Hertz

I encourage you to seek God every day by praying, "Lord God, please guide me in the right direction, always and forever." Miracles can happen within you, and *are* happening all around you.

I hope you pray regularly, and make prayer an act of honest surrender and confession. God is our Father who made this universe, made us—and we need to connect and talk with him often. Lord, I'm sold out for you lock, stock and barrel. I give you everything, because if I even keep a little piece, I'll mess it up! (Though the Lord reminds me I have to accept that in him I am made whole. Every day, I must train myself to be thankful that through God's grace within me, I am sufficient.)

> **Let us therefore come boldly to the throne of grace,**
> **that we may obtain mercy and find grace to**
> **help in time of need.**
> —Hebrews 4:16

We are God's children. He loves us with a love that we do not fully understand or even begin to fathom. We have help and hope because of his son, Jesus Christ, and the Holy Spirit. We have free will, the choice, whether we make use of the grace God offers.

Father God, we draw our strength from you. Hallelujah!

". . . But Jesus answered him, saying, "It is written, 'Man shall not live by bread alone, but by every word of God.'"—Luke 4:4

"Believers, look up—take courage.
The angels are nearer than you think."
—Billy Graham

Jesus sent an angel to tell me I was loved at ten years old. I really needed to hear that I was loved. It was so amazing how God let me know. And this is also true: when you're "sold out for Jesus" in this world you gotta' have hair; grow a thick hide; have some guts—because some people won't believe you! It may even feel like a few feathers are plucked from you by people who ridicule when you share your Christian experiences, act openly on your faith, and try to walk-the-walk. It's okay, just pray for them.

In Jesus Christ, every day we can make it a habit to stand strong on God's word. God is faithful to hear our prayers and act on his promises. The Bible is just as powerful, influential, and relevant in our world today as it was when God, the prophets and Jesus spoke it into existence. With it, we have the same authority as those whom we read about in the Bible. They were people, just like you and me, yet God listened and cared.

I pray these things for you:

- *Accept* God's heritage: You are part of the family.
- *Trust* God's word and put it to good use: It's God's power, not our power, but he lets us use it.
- *Speak* God's word in faith: Use it to further the Kingdom of God.
- *Claim* God's word for victory and protection: God is with you and will never leave you.

- **Understand** his promises: Live each day knowing they are true and intended for your life.
- **Ask** God to help you pray; ask him for what you need: You are good enough, just as you are.
- **Rest** in victory, peace and protection: Relationship with God, faith in who he is and what he does is an amazing way to live. I have tried everything else! Now I pray. It works.

Our timing and God's timing, our desires and God's desires for us, are often not the same, but *all* prayers are answered. He knows best and he is in control. I wish I had a dime for every time I've said, "Wow! That prayer was answered!"

> **"God proved His love on the Cross.**
> **When Christ hung, and bled, and died, it was**
> **God saying to the world, 'I love you.'"**
> —Billy Graham

I believe every God-inspired word in the Bible. Through Jesus, it is the *living* word of God. It is not dead, it does not change, nor does it return to you void. The Bible is number one on my "bestseller" list.

To endure in life takes strength and tenacity anyway, so go ahead and speak out for Jesus as you live each day. You could save a life—first yours, then someone else's. "*Wow, amazing!*" That can't be said too many times.

> **"Courage is contagious. When a brave man takes a**
> **stand, the spines of others are stiffened."**
> —Billy Graham

The miracles of God—his amazing grace within the chapters of this book, are still going on in my life today. Faith is an adventurous spiritual journey, especially the way I've gone about it—*Alaska style!* Never dull, and through it all God's confirmed he loves me anyway, just the way I am. *Halleluiah!*

I pray you see miracles in your life. I pray you feel God's unconditional love, joy and peace as it pours onto you today. Keep on in your life journey, your spiritual journey toward eternal life, with a grateful heart. Life doesn't get any better that!

The chapters in this book tell about my life and my spiritual journey with a magnificent God! Come up to Alaska, it's also a magnificent creation of God! We'd love to have you visit, but much bigger and more important is that you visit *with* God. We can't limit him, or what we can ask of him in our life, and what we can actually do and be—as we trust in him!

Thank you for letting me share with you what God has done for me *and with me,* and how he has been there during every bit of my life, even when I didn't know it. He is always there for you.

And it doesn't stop here—there are many more stories and chapters that will go on in my life and yours—*let's pass them on*—the message of belief and trust in a real, always present God.

He is with us, even when we may feel we don't deserve it. A good future belongs to you, a believer in Jesus Christ.

God's word is alive, angels are near, and the family of God is growing!

Thank you, Lord Jesus. Amen.

Erwin Hertz
http://www.ErwinHertzSr.com